COPING
WITH
DEPRESSION

COPING
WITH
DEPRESSION

WHILE SERVING GOD AND MAN

it's all true and still going on

M. H. MORROW

authorHOUSE®

AuthorHouse™
1663 Liberty Drive
Bloomington, IN 47403
www.authorhouse.com
Phone: 1-800-839-8640

Published by AuthorHouse   03/28/2012

ISBN: 978-1-4685-7448-7 (sc)
ISBN: 978-1-4685-7455-5 (e)

Any people depicted in stock imagery provided by Thinkstock are models, and such images are being used for illustrative purposes only.
Certain stock imagery © Thinkstock.

This book is printed on acid-free paper.

Because of the dynamic nature of the Internet, any web addresses or links contained in this book may have changed since publication and may no longer be valid. The views expressed in this work are solely those of the author and do not necessarily reflect the views of the publisher, and the publisher hereby disclaims any responsibility for them.

September 3, 2005

I'm still not sleeping well. When I lie down—God I'm so tired, my eyes are heavy, but once I turn the television off, I immediately wake up.

At this writing I'm at Nick's football game. I keep telling myself that I'm not a soccer mom, but I like being able to support Nick As I look at all the parents here, I get scared. It seems like I stick out like a sore thumb because the women just look at me, but the men look and speak and try to hold conversation. I hear Nick's team in the back ground saying their team cheer. The game starts at 2:30pm.

The day is not over I'm sure I'll have more to write. Nick's team won their game, Nickolas is telling me he feels good. I'm very proud of him; the coaches let him play all four quarters.

We are home now and everyone is relaxed. Cooking spaghetti for dinner turned out pretty good; I burned the cheese bread.

OK, let's try this thing normal humans call sleep!

September 4, 2005

I did not sleep at all last night. I tried not to look at the clock. All I'm thinking is that I'm glad I don't have to go to work. Because I would be in tears. OK it's 8:30 am Sunday morning. I'm telling myself to get up.

I'm up.

Ok, now get in the shower, get make-up on, do hair. Get Charlee and Nick so they can get ready. At the pace I'm moving we will miss breakfast at church. 10:45 on the dot. Made it.

Um . . . It's very emotionally awkward in service today. Everyone is drowned from the sickening news of category five Katrina. Ah, It's nice to know that Haaj has been transferred to Grambling State inland Louisiana. I found that out through the sermon. Service is over. I'm glad I came. Nick and Charlee want to go to the park, gas is $3.09/gallon, I have to conserve. My body is shutting down. I hate to lie down. No television I tell Nick and Charlee. One hour 30 minute nap, I feel good. Let's go for a walk guys. You've been good while mommy took a nap. Mommy can we spend the night at Miss Hicks house? Sure, let me call her when we get home. Miss Hicks says yes. We eat dinner. They pack their clothes. My body is trying to shut down. I'm back home. I take a shower.

Now I would love to have some male company. That's what my mind is telling me, but physically, it's another story. Now let's try this activity normal humans call sleep!

September 5, 2005

Again, sleep eluded me. I got out of bed at 9:30am. I had breakfast with M. at about 10:30am. I left the restaurant at 11:47am. We drove to Piedmont Park and lied on a blanket under a shade tree. We had very pleasant conversation, and of course, things began to get a little heated. We both agreed to stop, as he had a prior engagement with his nephew.

M. was adamant about seeing me later. He wants me to spend the night at his house. My answer was, of course, yes.

At 2:30 we left the park. I picked up Nick and Charlee by 3:30 or 4:00. We had a lot of fun at my father's annual barbeque. M. called; he's very excited about tonight, so am I. I'm finding myself to be kind of nervous, but also, extremely excited.

7:00pm, I'm on my way to my friends barbeque. I had fun and I got a chance to see her children, grandchildren, and her only son—beautiful family with lovely features. OK, by body is starting to shut down. I've got to get my children home before I get cranky. I'm home. Maurice is calling. I'll write more later.

Wow! I'm at M.'s house. Because I've decided too start keeping a daily journal, I must write of my experience. Why? you ask, because there will be days when I will be absolutely miserable with cluttered thoughts and the blackest depression that I would not wish on my worst enemy. And I would like to turn and read these pages to feel better.

Before I get to M.'s house, he explained to me that he is living in a house that is being renovated and that he only occupies three rooms. So of course, I expected menial furniture, but I was pleasantly surprised, it was very well furnished, very clean, very romantic. He looked great when he opened the door and he smelled so clean, skin soft, fresh breath, hands clean, soft. We were both very anxious, so I asked to relax a bit. I drank some water.

Then he looked at me, and kissed me softly. Oh he had tiny little lights, the size of candles strategically placed so the whole aura of his living quarters had a gothic romantic dark look about it. When he kissed me, he swept me off my feet like I was a feather and slowly carried me to his bed. Very plush blankets and pillows, dark red in color, jazz was playing in the background, he is defiantly a man of his word, he kissed me everywhere, from literally the top of my head and every toe. I felt a cold sensation on my tummy. Some kind of way he'd gotten some whip cream and put some at the edge of my purple thongs and began liking it off. Now, mind you, I'm still fully clothed and so is he. The foreplay was absolutely breath taking.

So, I'm lying on my back totally in the control of someone else and whip cream is now on my nipples. Right about now, I'm about to have a religious experience. I mean he's literally, to this as clean as possible, eating, licking, and sucking me like he has been derived of anything sweet since childhood. Then my pants come off, well . . . he take them off. Now, I'm going to be honest, at the age of 40, I've never experienced the pleasure of whip cream on my body. So now the whip cream is, well . . . take a guess . . . and he's definitely having his way with me. I softly tell him to stop because of what's about to happen, he stops and holds me. I then notice that he is still clothed but extremely excited. Oh yeah, I'm saying in my mind. I like what I feel. Are you OK? He asks. I'm fine. He starts kissing me very intensely, my spaghetti strap purple shirt comes off. Oh God, I hear myself say in my mind. I'm totally undressed. Then I whisper to him please be gentle. I will, he whispers back. He tells me to lay on top of him and kiss him. I'm trying to listen to his body and I think he wants me to undress him. Like he did for me, I take my time. He smells so good. I softly kiss his neck. Ahh, Jackpot! Then his nipples, OK this is working. Then I gracefully slide down and slip his pants off, boxer shorts, that is so sexy. I start licking him just below his navel and very close to his manhood, but never there. I'm not good at that so I don't want to ruin the moment.

He is staring to sweat and calling my name—pronouncing it correctly, I might add, which is always a turn on for me. He tells me to come and be on top of him. I oblige him. Now, in my mind I'm thinking please be gentle, very nice male equipment. He is gentle, he grabs me by my hips and enters me and tells me to look at him in the eyes, I say no. Look at me in the eyes, he says again. No, I say (that's a rule I have, no eye contact). Then he holds me really tight, flips me over, now I'm on my back and he's on top. Needless to say, we are having a very intense, vocal sweaty moment. I can tell that he's looking at me, but I'm kissing his arm.

He says again, "Menasha, look at me." I ignore him. He grabs my face to his so I could have contact with him. I'll leave to the imagination the things he was saying. Again, very intense moment—constant movement and kissing. I hear myself call his name several times. My body is now experiencing the pleasure it needs. I'm in a total zone completely soaked with sweat, probably two pounds of it. Are you OK?, he asks. "Fine," I say. "Am I satisfying you," he asks me. "Yes. More than you know"

Now, I notice that he's still within himself. He is so sensual, his self-control is serious turn on for me. The longer he goes, I can hang right with him. He gives me water to drink. He's rubbing my hair. Then he massages me with shea butter.

He starts to kiss me everywhere. His mouth is so warm; again, he is so attentive and he has definitely found my weakness. Now, I'm going to be honest. When a man knows how to kiss a girl in that particular place and get it right, it can drive you crazy, so I've taught myself to say strong.

OK, it's time for me to reverse this. I tell him I want to show him something. "Keep doing what you're doing" I say to him. "Don't stop till I say," he listens. There's a certain thing I noticed my body does at a certain point in sexual activity. When this happens with me, a man can no longer contain himself.

I whisper to him to stop. "Let me put my legs on your shoulders."

"OK" he says.

Now, this position that he's in, I know that he can't contain himself. I have complete control now, and I'm on my back. Now, he is truly in another world. I love it when I hear a man give a deep throaty moan. He's sweating profusely. "I" give him very intense eye contact and I put my thumb in his mouth, and I start to move my hips.

Oh God, this is damn good, very erotic, but I want him to let go before I do, I move my hips more forcefully. The muscles in his arms have tensed up. He is looking at me. I tell him, "Let go, let it go." Ahh, that deep throaty sound of release coming from a man is absolutely beautiful.

I experience my release from his reactions and we are in total relaxation. With the soft sound of jazz and low lights I don't' know about him but I fell asleep for about two hours. I feel him rubbing my back and kissing the nape of my neck. Then I hear birds signing. Oh my God! It's six o'clock am. I've got to go. He walks me to the car and kisses me. I have to be at work by eight he says. But I'll be OK. I kiss him and we part company.

September 6, 2005

Wow let me get Nick and Charlee to the train station, 6:25 am. I stop at Krystal's to get two sunrisers before going back home. I eat one, crawl into my bed by 6:45am. Dammit! Who is calling me at 7:46am? Cell and

Home number, I check, it's W., then Captain Adger, then Miss C., then a Martron sister. I'm somewhere between delirious now. I feel like I'm Hallucinating. C. calls twice more. She is about the only person besides my parents and children that I would interrupt something for. I call her, her daughter N is blind. I'll help her I say. But please I beg of you, let me close my eyes. I didn't get home until 6:00am. We hung up, we'll we did talk for a while. Then I called N. By this time, it's twelve noon. She said she would call me back in 30 minutes.

We hang up, then I lied down. I couldn't move anymore. My body can't take this. I drift off and on. I'm very relaxed, caught between consciousness I hear everything going on outside, but I can't move. I think that I'm afraid to let myself sleep.

OK, it's now 4:30pm. Get up. Take a shower. Start dinner. Nick and Charlee will be here at 5:15pm.

Shower felt good, dinner is being prepared. I take Nick to football practice. I get Charlee settled for bed. Nick gets home at 8:45pm. He's very responsible when it comes to certain things. He eats its dinner. I ask him about football practice. He says that he didn't even break a sweat.

Now my house is quite. Everyone is settled. I call M. He sounds pleased that I call. We talk for about 20 minutes. He says that he can't wait to see me again, to rekindle the pass of last night. I say OK. I tell him I don't want to keep him on the phone. I know he has to get up for work. I hang up, turn the television off, and guess what, I fall into a deep sleep.

September 7, 2005

Oh God I slept so good! I feel refreshed. By 6:15am I have Nick and Charlee at the trains station at a normal time. Afterwards, I go to Krystal's to get my sunrisers. I eat one, get back into bed, and fall asleep for an hour. That's good though, I have to see my doctor today.

I get out of bed at 10:30am. I refuse to look at the tele, the aftermath of category 5 Katrina is still strong. By 11:30 I'm ready. At 11:45, I'm on the road. I arrive at 12:30. At 1:00 o'clock the office manager asks me, "can I help you?" The doctor didn't write down that I had an appointment, but she remembered that I had one.

As always, information is pulled from me. Everything went well though. I still can't quite relax on that "sofa" and the environment is very pleasant. She's pleasant to talk to. "I'm still not sleeping" I told her. She suggested melatonin (a natural sleep aid). On the ride back home, I went backwards, I realized it when I was in Coweta County. But I usually take the street way back and this time I took the expressway.

I stopped at Public's and got the sleep aid. I'm not going to take it tonight because I drank a wine good. I don't want any side effects. Nick is home from football practice. He has a game next Thursday and Saturday. Charlee and me ate dinner. Now Nick is going to a.

I'm very sleepy and I hope I will fall into as deep a sleep as last night. Tossing and turning, it's 11:45pm. Maybe I will take one of those melatonins.

Whoa! It's working. 12:30pm at night. I'm sleeply. I hope I didn't get the wrong dosage, it was 2 dosage amounts, 300mg and 3g. I bought the 3 grams. OK, I'm outta here.

September 8, 2005

I feel groggy as hell. I believe the doc told me not to take the melatonin too late. Got Nick and Charlee at the regular time. Got my sunrisers. Got back in bed, looked at the weather channel. I did fall back to sleep.

Wating for capret clearner, had to call them. They showed up at 11:00 o'clock. Left the house, at 11:30 I'm at the gym. By, 11:45 I've had a great workout. Sitting in the sauna by myself, got my peppermint oil. God this feels good. Leaving now at 1:45pm.

Feeling a bit dark, I don't want to go home but I need to cook a good meal for myself and the children. I'm home. I check mail. I'm officially on short term disability.

I'm having quality time for myself. Actually, my house is clean. It's quite outside this is kind of nice, I now need to fully focus on regrouping for when I go back to work. I'm definitely going and circulate my resume.

The group that The kids are home dinner is being prepared, salmon crocketts, rice, and plantains. Umm, that's good. Nick his home early from football. If all I had known, we could have eaten with the all together.

Ms G. called me. She's a very sweet lady. I like how calm she is. She was concerned about my health.

Sis Strong called me, she's one of my matron sisters. She gave me a case of biscuits. I'll share them with my parents.

I texted W. a break-up message I can't see him anymore, even though we weren't a couple. Basically, at this time in my life I get lonely for companionship. I'm tired of sleeping alone in my bed.

M. has called several times. I'm ignoring him. I called him today and he acted like he was bothered by my call. As I write this, W is calling. I peeped his routine sometime ago. It's 10:30pm. He will call me every other night at this time like he's been told to go to the store and get something, which gives him free time to call me.

I'll miss him a great deal. Talk about a fine black man. And he was FINE IN BED. His message says that he didn't know we had a problem and he wants to talk to me personally.

M. Just called and we talked for 17 minutes. It's amazing how men come out with the truth when you catch them in their shit. He says that there was a female and some of her things are still at his house. And the relationship ended not too long ago. I told him I would back off if he's still dealing with her. He says not to worry about it. I tell him women can be knuckle heads and I don't do drama.

It's 11:00pm. I'm tired. I'm going to take a melatonin. I feel grouchy. I hope I sleep.

September, 9, 2005

I think I slept, I'm not sure . . . well . . . I can't remember, because I'm writing this entry on the date of September 10th.

Now, let's see, I got my hair done at touch-up. The doctor called me, the primary care doctor. I have to make an appointment. Nick didn't have football practice.

I didn't get home until a little after 7:00pm. Nick and Charlee were outside playing. I made them take a shower, then we rode to Mickey Dee's and I paid Ms. H.

I talked on the phone to Mrs. G.

Oh God! I know my day was productive. Let me think, oh yeah, I paid car note, bought groceries, and paid other bills.

I did go to the gym, that felt good. W called me. I refuse to call him back. OK took a melatonin. I remember felling anxious.

September 10, 2005

I didn't sleep at all. Just as I dosed, Charlee started coughing and she caoughed all night. I think her stuffed animals may be the cause.

I'm now officially up at 7:30am. I finally get out of the bed at 8:15am. First thing I do is call Captain Adams at home to make sure that he has all of documentation, "he does."

I get Nick and Charlee something to eat. Then my Saturday treat to myself, breakfast at beautiful restaurant. I ask my best friend if she would like to go with us to our church pick-nick. We get to the place at about 1:30pm. I introduce her to my church family (If that's what you want to call them).

Everyone asks about Haji. Oh, guess what, he's at Fisk Univeristy. I can't bare to have anyone else ask me about him or tell me anything about him, because I'm convinced that he hates me. I don't know what I've done wrong. Again, I'm not paranoid, but people at church look at me really judgmental when it comes to him. God help me to remain Christian like.

My day is winding down, I have to get away from these church people. Ms J is really showing her true self. She's constantly looking in my mouth, but she doesn't speak to me.

I found that I can't take this atmosphere anymore. I tell C. She suggests we take a walk. Great idea!

We walked to the firefighters activities, saw some very handsome men. I got a ride on a beautiful thoroughbred male horse name Jr. I was having very fond memories of living in Arizona and talking day trips and half day trips on horseback at the hole in the wall ranch. The guides name was Hooker, his nick name was happy hooker, because he was always in good spirits.

The guy with the horse today knew the place well and he make my ride last long.

Well our church function is over. As we are walking back down to the recreation center, pastor D and his wife are leaving. I politely wave and I'll leave it at that, but never again will I ask this church to help me with anything.

I drop off Nick and Charlee at home so that they can relax before their father picks them up. Ms. C needs to stop at the store. Afterwards, I take her home.

I ask her how I should handle cheating. Her advice, which was bitterly accepted, but I needed to hear it was "he's being spiteful, and he's making you look like boo boo the fool." She's right. She goes on to say that everyone knows she is but me, let him go.

My ride back home was quick, Charlee calls she wants me to come home she misses me, I have got to learn to except my two youngest schildren's love. They care for me so much. I feel the same about them, but I feel numb and clouded by something. God, could it be el Haaj, could it be elena, could it be Marium, what the hell is wrong with me?

I texted leandra to let her know that Haaj is at Fisk, not gambling as I suspected, Lena calls.

I think that I shall write a letter and express to her how I feel my holdest three children have been lied to by her and her dead son. At this time I'm anxious, angry, depressed, hurt, sorrowful, paranoid, deeply saddened, and I think I might be tired. But I know I'm not going to sleep. I want to ready my Bible but I don't' have faith right now. I feel as though it doesn't exist.

Nick and Charlee love their father so much. They were very glad to see him. Charlee jumped in her father's arms and held him so tight. I really hope that he will be able to take care of them if something happens to me. I don't quite trust him. I will always question the woman he chose to leave me for. Unfortunately, she doesn't care for my little ones.

Damit I can't relax. The tele is on, my room light is on, I think I'm going to sleep with the light on tonight. Should I call Lena, should I write her a letter, ignore her phone call? Jeez, she's close to 80 years old. I have a soft spot for my elders but I still have wounds from 3 years ago. The British comedies are making me relax a little. I'll stop there and try to get comfy. I hope I sleep. I feel like I'm going to die a lonely person. I can't be as horrible as I'm feeling lately.

September 11, 2005

Well I did sleep off and on, I got up about 2:30am. Turned my roof light off, I kept the tele on. I finally got out of my bed at 8:30am got ready for church. Long day at church the sermon was excellent. Everything Jonah felt I wrote last night—the gist of the sermon was don't get angry and trust your faith. I was angry this morning, but I'm glad I went to church. Matron's meetings was 3 long hours, we got a lot accomplished. My dinner was delicious me and Rosie White Hosted.

$435 has been collected so far I hope 200 more appears.

I think C. is angry at me I thought I told me it cost 7 dollars.

Nick and Charlee are home in in bed school tomorrow I'm sleepy but looking at the crazy ass movie Stephen Kind Rose Red I'll take a melatonin and hopefully fall asleep.

September 12, 2005

I did fall asleep, a good deep sleep. I kept the curtain open. The outside street lamp was comforting.

I am now convinced that my name sas been smeared at church. Sister Walton has been very gracious in handling that matter for me I umust get shi matrons' a card and her a chard separately. I will never ask the church for help again. My motto at work is when black people are in charge os something shit alswasy goes on. And thatis is seemling true at providence Baptish church. I'm going to agree with sister zinger, she said something that was so profound last night—"I didn't join the preacher, I joined the church" I'll have to look at it that way.

I truly believe that his messages are God sent, But I also have to understand that he's only a man and he still has sinful as he is weak to gossip—I've always known this.

I've expressed my disappointment with Bro reed and both church secretaries on how this matter is beings taken care of. I'm sure it's gotten back to the pastor.

Nick got in trouble. A parent called me and said that nick was punching her hchild in the face and busted his lip. I gave her Charles number and they talked. Nick is out of Football fo rhte season. That's my rule in my house. Idon't know why he can't seem to say way from trouble. We had left for dinner tasted and great and we ate together like we used to. I went to the self service care wash and had a great workout at the gym. I feel my body developing again. I'm going to miss the gym when I go back to work. I'm not missing work at all. Damnit I need to win the lottery! I'm reading a great book, The Divinci Code. It's making me think, something I haven't done for a while.

Well I'm winding down I feel Ok I guess, kinda unsure. I must also focus on my faith, read the bible, psalms 119 and 92 help me. I'm going to take a melatonin, I hope its not addictive.

September 13th,

Didn't sleep last night my mind was in overdrive. I let the dr. read my jounal, I'll ask her about that tomorrow. I seem to express my feelings better in writing. OK it's 7am, I need to meet sister Walton at 8am. It's

8am, we both pulled in the lot at the same time, She counts the money out to me, $480, she goes with me to get the money order. In two years at Centra Villa apts I've never been laste with my retn. I write the manager a letter and tell him that his is all I could pay. I drop the letter in the drop box. I go ups stairs to my apt, take a bath, now I'm wondering what to think. Well I have a full thank of gas, so I decide to go and lay out in the park and read. This is nice.

Before I go back to work, I must update my resume so I can circulate it other departments at TBS.

OK, I'm getting sleep out here, I know a glass of wine at Mellowmushroom is $10, I think, I have $10, why not. UM . . . nice and chilled. Ok time to focus on things I need to do. See the doc Wednesday, firday get the 15,000 mile checkup on my car and on the weekend do something special just me and the children.

Nick has in school suspension, charlee arrived home at 5:30pm. We had quality time. She read to me part of her homework assignment. Erica came by to see me. She tells me she's fired. Ms S. resigned, she's moving back to Florida. She goes on to say people are getting written up everyday for bullshit reasons. I meediately start stressing and I change the subject and ask her how school is going for her. Just as she was about to answer, nick arrives home at 730. She says that she doesn't want to keep me long. Nick and I talk a little after she leaves, then we eat dinner.

The children are in bed. The house is quite I'm at ease I read the bible I have the tele on. I'll try to sleep.

September 14, 2005

Damit, why didn't' I sleep? Oh well I'm up at 5:15 am I wait for the children we're all dressed I'm trying to stay on schedule for when I returned to work. They're at the train station. I'm back home I'm lying down I'm not relaxed, paster durley calls the cell and home. I don't answer because I didn't know the number. I never listen to the answering machine unless it continually blinks. I call the church at 930 the secretary says that he's at a funeral. At 1030 I'm on my way to the gym I need a good work out. I pack everything I need to change and do my hair and makeup at the gym. Apt at 2pm.

Workout was great I feel good, while in the sauna I find myself thinking about M. Umm nice thoughts very vivid I would be so nice to have him make love to me. I've done 30 min in the sauna, shower and home by 1pm. I'm on the road, I really love this drive, it's open, green, not too many black people Houses spaced out, I could live out here. At the dr.'s—damn why do I feel so tense all of the sudden?

Fist thing I notice, the doc has a nice rinse in her hair it looks good on her. I ask if she could read my journal, she agress that she'll do that. Um again . . . she has to pull information out of me Her questions strike me in a strange emotional way—good I guess. Sometimes, I feel myself becoming cold. She asks about my social life. I thought about M. I told her about finding out I was adopted at the age of 33, that really plays with my mind. She had an interesting concept that I had thought about once before. Maybe I'll try it. Tomorrow I'll have my prescription for Paxil, I'm nervous about taking it, but I know its better. Ok. I'm winding down my phone's ringing. It's Daren, a friend, we talk about movies and stuff but he wants more. I cannot! He reminds me too much of my brother.

September 15th

I was relaxed, but I didn't sleep. I'm up at 5:45am, kids at the trainstation by 615. I'm back home laying down I dose off. Phone rings at 8:30. It's pastor D. I explain my rent situation And he says so you only need $200 more? He's says that he's going to have breakfasat with LF, but that he'll call me after. We hang up. I try to dose off but I just lay there. It's 11am. If I continue to do this, I'll sink back into the black void. GET UP!

Where should I go? I look for a copy of my resume in my briefcase. Damn I can't find a copy. Well, next option, this is my day off from the gym. I could go to east Atlanta. I'll be close to pick up the kids. Nick as to weigh in for the game at 5:15pm, there' no way he'd make it on the bus.

I drive to this restaurant in east Atlanta called the flat iron. My kinda place in the daytime, at night, I think not. I have a salad and a glass of Charonday. My book is very interesting. I'm buzzing off of one glass of wine, what a feeling.

I call my best friend Collins, she lives down Moreland. She joins me and orders some hotwings. Umm those are good, she agrees. I say to myself Thank God my buzz in dying down. WE have a good talk, we haven't talked since Sunday.

It's 330 time to go. Nick comes right out at 4pm Charliee at 4:07. I get Nick to his weigh in right at 5:00pm While driving I get a call drom Dr M's office. I have to see someone at the behavioral clinic before I can get Paxil. My heart drops. Does this mean I can't see my dr. anymore. No, she says it's just procedure.

In my mind I'm thinking that it's taking an act of Congress for me to get this medication. I'd like to have in my system for a bit before I got back to work with a 9mm on my side. Shit I'm pissed! Ok, don't panic, call the dr. tomorrow.

I wonder how Nick's game is going? I hope that he gets to play. Even though Nick seems to stay in mischief he's a very sensitive child. His feelings get hurt easily. I told him when I dropped him off not be be surprised if he can't play since he got in trouble at school. The reason I didn't' want to say. When he's benched he looks up at me so pitifully. It breaks my heart. I suppose Nick well be here shortly. I'm groggy. I hope I sleep, I'm going to have a melatonin.

September 16th,

My body is going through that phase again, I don't' sleep no matter what I do. If anything kills me it wil be madness from insomnia! I didn't sleep last night, I didn't even dose off. 5:45 am, were' all up, kids are at the trainstation on time, I'm back home staring at the ceiling until 10:30.

Get UP! The void is gonna get you! I get my gym bag ready I can't remember what I did from then till noon, but I started by workout at noon. It's taking me a minute to get into it, Ok focus focus, there's only two other people in here, perfect, not crowded, nice rhythm to the music, stretch, OK stretch again. Now go to the weights, workout, workout, workout! It was great, I'm now in the sauna, Oh God this is pure joy very relaxing, completely naked, alone, the smell of peppermint oil and heat.

My 30 min. is over I take a good hot shower, 2pm. I go to C.'s house. She has great news, a promising job-interview on Wednesday, I'm happy for her. I arrive home, the kids are here, we arrive at the same time. Nick has football practice and a boy scout trip tomorrow overnight I'm going to take Charlee to Miss Hick's house while Nick is gone for the weekend.

I may think about calling Maurice, I probably need to release some other kinds of stress. But, I'll think about it. Well let me take another shower, I feel sticky. Charlee is sitting on the steps with LL's daughter and the neighbor's niece. I called by brother to wish him a happy birthday, I'm sure he'll get the message on Monday for he wasn't at work today. I haven't seen him since 1998. I don't think he'll be back in Atlanta anytime soon, especially with the news we received that year.

Well that's all for now, I hope I sleep.

September 17th

I usually wait unless much later in the evening to write, but I need to write. I didn't sleep at all last night. I feel cranky as hell we're all up at 830 and we give the house a very thorough cleaning. We have breakfast by 10:25, we leave for church, there's an even going on in the church parking lot, there's familiar cars. Brother R hesitantly comes over to speak to me I don't even look at him, I just answer that everything is good and give a smile. The last time we spoke, a week ago, I asked him in parking lot what was going on since I has having problems getting an answer from the church in terms of my rent situation. He asked if I told the pastor, I said I did. He asked if decon M is helping, I said yes. He's on the finance committee he said, you'll be OK. At that moment I felt a surge of anger, And I said "If something is going on here I need to know" He gave me a strange but knowing look. Don't get angry he says, "hold on to your faith" as I'm backing out of the parking lot. As I drive home I get really pissed off. Sis W. Finance committee, what the hell is, you know what, forget it! Hell no how can she not go to the pastor and explain to him my situation she's on the finance committee!!! Sometimes It literally takes a brick to hit me upside the head before I realize what I've know all along. I don't know what El has got them thinking. I've done nothing to that boy. In the end, I just need to turn the situation over to God. As my mind comes back, Bro R walks off, realizing that I'm not going to engage in further converstion. I tell myself I'm so glad I never slept with him and it didn't take abrick for me to know that would have been a big mistake. Preachers, black preachers that is, tend to preach about what they do, especially if it involves sex or drinking. At 11am the scout master finally shows up, Nick is excited, Charlee starts to look sad they really lover eachother and hate to be apart for more than a day. I take Charlee to Miss H's house, I give her 3 dollars for candy and chips. She perks up, I'll call and check on her in a couple of hours, I say to myself, I watch her go in and I drive away.

My off centeredness began as I was leaving the Ihop on Peachtree. Oh my goodness, too many black people, too much noise, I've got to get to east Atlanta.

I'm driving, my mind is running wild Shit I'm going to scream! I feel like I want to cry maybe I should check myself into the emergency room that way I can get this damn medication. I'm starting to tremble a bit. What the hell is going on with me. OK music 102.5, turn it loud, block out all this rap shit I'm hearing. Take the street way, If I get on the expressway, I'll loose track of how fast I'm going and be at 90 before I know it. I've done that before when my mind was racing, I didn't realize it until I was passing everyone. Oh God I'm here. There it is the library a nice quite spot. I've fallen in love with east Atlanta, it's very bohemian mostly Caucasian. A few black people, but not many. I like that way. OK I'm in the library where I can see outside as well as inside. So I'm sitting for about 45 minutes, finally relaxed writing these words And this man comes over. I must have given him a look because he dropped his smile like "oh damn is she gona curse me out" so I softened my expression. He says "Hi we came in together, I'm over there using the computer because mine at home has a glitch" I'm thinking, how long should I engage this conversation, but he has a kind voice. I said maybe it has a virus. He said, no it's a . . . . some computer word. I said OK, I hope you get that fixed. We talked for about 20 min. He's still standing but getting comfortable, I think, I know this comfort level, he's about to ask me my name. By the way, he says, my name is A. What's yours? Menasha. Oh, what language is that? Hebrew I say. I also tell him the meaning. He tells me the meaning an origin of his name. I'm thinking please don't ask for my number. Your're so not my type. He was very thin older man terrible hands all knotted and walked like he had a bad back. If he asks, I'll give my usual "I'm married" line and show him the ring on my left hand.

"Well Meneeshia" Menasha I say. "I hope to see you again" I say, "have a good day, I hope you fix your computer." He walked away.

Fewww I sight with relief. I'm finally at ease. I feel I can handle outside. I hear a live band playing. It's such a beautiful day. I'll work on my resume later at home.

I take a quick walk through the streets and there seems to be some sort of neighborhood event going on. Not quite up to the atmosphere like I thought. But I stop and look at the authentic Mexican hamocks on display. It's times like these that I wish I still owned my house. Well, I don't have $59 or two trees so I might as well keep going. I stop at the store to get a soda and some popcorn. I drive home. Just as I get relaxed, CJ calls. This is an old aquiantance. An off and on relationship for 7 years. The last time I was with him was 6 months ago, the last time we talked was 3 weeks ago. Well, it was really a text. I texted, "have a safe labor day" he replied "thx u 2"

CJ is asking me out for a date. I immediately said no. Our dates always ended in sex. But he's no good. So I'd end up with an excellent meal and be sexually frustrated. But there's one thing that I taught him to do quite well, but I was adamant that I was in for the day. And as CJ does, he said "I'll be there at 730 to pick you up" NO CJ! He hangs up. Shit, I take a shower, curl my hair and put on something simple. At 730pm I hear him reaving his Porshe engine. He knows that I don't allow him to come up anymore, so that's the way he lets me know that he's here.

He opens the passenger door for me as he always does. You look good Menasha. Thanks I say. Good to see you, he says. Where do you want to go?

You invited me CJ I say. Just as long as we go to a restaurant. No detours. I tell him that I'd love to have a healthy green salad. We go to a great restaurant in the downtown college park area. The salad was outstanding, I had a glass of wine. He tried to persuade me to have another. NO I said, CJ I'm fine.

We take a nice walk around the area. He holds my hand. "Now this isn't so bad is it Menasha" he says.

No I say. And then he says, well why is it that when I've wanted to touch you on other occasions, you cringe?

CJ I said We've been though this before. Let's not. He agrees.

It's 9pm Remember I said. I wanted to be home by 9. We drive back to my place. He walks me to the door and I tell him thank you for a nice evening. He looks at me. Sooo, you're not going to invite me in.

No I say.

He kisses me softly on the neck and gives me a long passionate hug. I felt myself totally relax in his arms and then I pulled away.

What did you do that Menasha? I could see that he was upset. I said I'm sorry I didn't mean to.

And then he says "Do you want me to leave?"

"Yes, no" I say. "I don't know" I turn away from him. He grabs me.

What's wrong Menasha?

Nothing I say. I hug him.

But this time I don't let go. Again I feel myself totally relax in his arms. Damn he feels good. He smells good. And then it happens. Something that took me totally off guard.

I start crying uncontrollably. He holds me tightly. "Baby what's wrong? Did I do something wrong?"

I noticed, he's genuinely concerned. He tells me to open the door and promises that we wont' go pass the dinning room. He sits on the black stool, I sit on the floor. He massages my neck and back. I apologize to him. It's OK he says. Anything you want to talk about? No I say.

CJ has always had the softest hands. A couple of minutes pass.

I tell him to come to my room. Are you sure? He asks.

Yes.

I need his familiar touch, he's terrible, but his touch and foreplay are so romantic. He continues to message my body he takes off my shirt and my pants. Oh God his hands feel so good. I feel myself becoming excited. He still has his clothes on. I unbutton his shirt. I feel myself become a little aggressive. I stop. Tonight I need to be the one on the submissive side. He tells me to relax and continues to message me. He's kissing me, his tongue is so far down my mouth I can hardly breathe. It feels good. He messages and kisses my breasts. He's all over me.

What do you want me to do he asks.

CJ I need you to give me an orgasm. I feel tears rolling down my face.

I didn't bring a condom he says. Then kiss me, I say. That's what I've taught him to do very well.

He lays on top of me, puts both hands above my head and he kissing me all over taking his time. He's very excited. But I know that without a condom, he won't penetrate me. I've always admired that about him.

I'm totally relaxed, enjoying his touch, the sound of the fan, the dim light through the window. Oh my goodness it's been a while, I hope I don't wake my neighbors. I start to breath heavy, he's holding me so tight, he's in total control. I'm sweating, his shirt is off. Tears are still rolling down my face and that terrific feeling is only seconds away! He's holding me even tighter, I can no longer contain my emotions. We catch eachother's eyes and I have an orgasm. I tell him to hold tight for a minute. I've gottcaha he says. I dose off for a while. I wake when I feel him going to the shower. I'm not going to stay because I don't want to confuse you he says. I agree.

"God you're beautiful Menasha" Come walk me to the door to you can lock it. And Please answer your phone tomorrow.

I will CJ.

He kisses me, I lock the door. Please God let me go back to sleep.

September 18th

I don't fall back to sleep. I tried everything, chair, sheep, nothing worked.

It's Sunday, I'm not going church and today is my day off from the gym. I drive to Piedmont Park to read by book and newspaper. I have no watch and I don't take my cell. I'm so tired I've lost track of time.

I'm sitting in a nice shady spot trying to keep my eyes open. What a beautiful day. It's so crsp. I love the fall in the south. Well, pretty soon I need to head back to pick up Nick and Charlee. Wait a couple of more minutes I tell myself. I'm staring to shut down, I can hardly move, no no get up. I've got to cook dinner, get uniforms ready. Damn what time is it?

I walk back to my car, groggy and hungry.

Everyone's picked up. They both need a bath. Nick, you smell like a baby elephant. He laughs when I say that.

So, how was your trip? We went fishing and swimming but I didn't catch anything. Charlee interjects, I stayed up till 11pm we watched scary movies she told Nick about Jeffery and Devin and Ellens' baby.

As they talked, I started dinner. I know Nick has to be hungry. I looked and listened to their conversation. I realized that they are happy children. I really start to regret this depression or whatever this is that I'm struggling with. It's hereditary. I'm wondering which of my children I've cursed with it. I only hope that I'm still lucid if my children need me.

Well dinner is read, it looks good smells good, chicken, rice, onions, and biscuits. I didn't realize I fixed this much. We eat and have conversation.

Charlee looks so sleepy, she's still stuffy. I tell her that before I buy her anything to take I want her natural defenses to help.

What's that?

I explain to her.

It's 7:45, time for bed. School tomorrow. By 8:30, the house is quiet, I don't lie down, I sit in my chair I watch Cartoon Network for a while. At 9:30 I take a melatonin, I hope I fall asleep.

September 19th

I didn't sleep. I tossed and turned all night. 5:45am, time to get up. I get Nick and Charlee to the train station, I'm so sleepy while driving. Please don't let me wreck. I almost feel like I'm dreaming. Back home now. I've got to lie down. I sleep for 1.5 hrs. It's 8:30 I'm hungry. I can't move. When I open my eyes again;, it's 10:30 and I'm hungreee! If I continue to lie here the day is gone. It's gym day. I get to the gym by 12:15 and I'm in the sauna by 1:15. The workout was good and the sauna feels good.

2:24 I'm working on my resume in the Library. I'm jittery as hell! I gota take a walk before I scream. At 4pm I head home. I'm sitting in a chair finishing the last pages of mybook. Great ending. I'm relaxed but I can't fall asleep. Nick and Charlee will be home soon.

Nick and Charlee get home at 5:30. No football practice today. Nick said that he heard that his team lost on Saturday. I said, see they probably lost because they needed you.

Yeah, he said, that's what I was thinking.

Poor Charlee, I'll have to take her the doctor she's still stuffed up.

Oh my head is throbbing. We eat dinner, the kids are in bed by 730. The phones are ringing. It's Ms. C and Ms. T. I'll call them tomorrow. I'm not in the mood.

8pm, I'm scared to lie down. I don't want to sit up. I don't know what to do. I have to go to bed because I have a long drive tomorrow to Conyers for maintenance on the car. OK, I'm going to sleep. I take a melatonin.

September 20th

I slept very little When I finally felt myself dose off. I jumped up. I thought I heard Charlee calling me. I went to check on her, both her and nick were out cold. By 4:30am I'm awake and miserable. At 6:15 I get Nick and Charlee to the train station. I have to get some sleep before this drive.

9am I'm late for my apt. I don't even know if I slept. I just know its 9am. By 930 I'm on the road, at the dealership by 10:00 and the car is done by 12:45. My head is throbbing! I think I have Charlee's cold, when I get home I'll take something. The drive home on 120 is hellacious. I've got to get off and find a street way home.

2:45, I'm home, I take an alka-selzer, I doze off. It's 5:30 the kids are home. They have choir practice. I feel like shit between my cycle, this cold, headache, clogged thoughts. I feel like I'm gona die.

As promised, I call Ms. T. She opened my eyes as to why the delay in help came from the church. She starts off: well you make $19/hr and you got 15,000 from selling the house so can you give back the money we gave you for rent?

I was speechless, what she said didn't register at first. Everything got queit. Finally I said, "Oh my God" What?

She kept talking. I swear I have no ideas what she was saying. I was an emotional fireball ready to say everything non-Christian. She talked to me for 4.56 minutes. I can only remember the first one minuite: $19/hr, $15,000, can you give me my money back?

I came back to my senses. I remember her saying . . . . "well it's late, I won't hold you. Tell the children hi and take care" Damn, I think I just came back from the twilight zone.

After we hung up I called Sis L., president of the matrons. I said "I just wanted to tell you that Pastor D. gave me a check for $200 for the rest of rent. Oh good she said. "Sis L, I need for you to squash something for me." She listened. I could hear by her quite "um"s that she had hear the same thing Ms. T had heard.

After I finished talking, her reply was, "Well, is it true?"

"Is it true? One of the reasons I joined the matrons was to be more lady like as I mature, but if I hear anymore of this I'm going to snap!"

She said, "Hold on Menasha, you need to have thick skin, whoever is point a finger at you as four more pointing at them"

OK I say

"No It's not true! And I'll never ask the church for anything else!"

My cell rings. It's Nick and Charlee. They're done with choir practice. I tell Sis. L I have get Nick and Charlee. She says to call her when I get back. I do—less than 7 minutes later. No answer. I try several times. No answer. I take a night time Alka-selzer for my stuffy nose and hope I sleep.

September 28th 2005

I saw the doctor today, she read my journal . . . Of course . . . she had questions.

"Out of all of your children, who has hurt you the most?"

"El-Haaj" I tell her.

She told me that I should write a letter to the children, the 3 oldest, and if I don't mail them, burn them after a week.

After the doctor, I had to go make a visit at the Drew Charter School. It seems like Charlee is being a smartass in class, not doing her work, and down right failing math class. Afterwards, I go home to try to relax, but instead I work on the shelves that D. gave me.

The kids are home, I'm glad to see them. Nick has a game in Cobb county. They won the game. My boy didn't get home till 10:30pm. He says the van broke down.

All of us had a very light dinner and went to bed.

September 29th

I didn't sleep last night. I've been driving the kids to school since the governor of GA decided that all kids should have two early snow days it didn't make sense to buy a Marta card. I went to the gym and had a great workout and the sauna felt great!

I went to little five points. Change of scenery, Jake's Pizza, very cool spot, had a $3 meal, worked on journal, left at 4pm. Got home at 4:30, going to spend a little quality time with myself.

I miss W. I broke down and called him. Shocked me and said that he's coming over tomorrow. He asked me why I broke it off with him, I told him that you can't stay overnight, come over late and you can't stay, I'm tired of that I tell him.

He's says that he's glad I called. "I miss you" he says, "When can I see you?"

Tomorrow I ask.

Well it will have to be late and you don't like that.

September 30th

Didn't sleep well last night but I was very relaxed. I was excited about being with Wes. I took Nick and Charlee to school stopped at Mickey Dee's: 2 hashbrowns and apple juice. Got home, back in bed, slept for about 2 hours.

October 4th

Well the past couple of nights I've been very relaxed but unable to go into a deep sleep. Wes and I are back into eachother. He is wonderful.

I'm back at the gym. I took about a week off because of that time of the month. It's so hard to get back into it, but I'll get there.

I was supposed to go with C. to the new Perry Homes and fill out an application but my body was shutting down and I was getting cranky and running low on car fuel.

I'm home now the children have eaten. I'm in my room, tiered, sleeply, cranky. I really think don't need medication but I guess I do.

October 5th

I didn't sleep well last night. I got up to get gas money from a co-worker. Kids were ready when I got back at 6:25am, by 6:30 they were at the station. I got back home by 7:05, phones kept ringing—I didn't answer either of them. I thought it was raining but it was the maintenance crew cutting grass. I had it really dark in the room. I lifted the curtain and the sky was blue and the sun was shining bright. I forced myself out of bed.

I got to the gym at 11:15am. I had a great 1 hr workout. Sauna felt great, but as I was leaving the gym I felt myself drowning again, quick.

I want to go home and sleep. But I don't want to go home. I don't know what I want.

I want to die actually. I'm so fucking unhappy. I feel like I'm not accomplishing anything. Everytime I get my finances together, a fucked up thing happens and I literally fall six months backwards. I mean Damn. Every time I saved a little stash of money, El-Haaj would find it. I mean Damn I had a nice chunk of change and cash stashed, you know, for emergencies. I was thinking that Nick and Charlee kept me from losing my mind but that's not working anymore. I've dropped off cooking good dinner time meals. I'm starting to look tired even though I work out. I called Wes and told him that I had something to do because I didn't have a physical desire to have him. At this writing I'm miserable. I need something good to happen, something positive, money, news, God to tell me to have a purpose, a good nights sleep. Another job, where I'm the boss, Freedom from everything.

Well I don't know what else to write. I have a doctor's apt. tomorrow and Friday.

I HATE MY LIFE!!!

October 6th, 2005

I didn't sleep at all. I wasn't going to let Nick and Charlee go to school but they woke up at 7:15 and we left the house at 8am. They got to school at 8:30.

I absolutely have no money at all. A negative $21 in my savings account. I get back home, eat a bowl of cereal and go back to bed. I sleep or something till 12:30. I get up, shower, leave and get to the doctor's at 2:10 for my 2:00pm appointment.

I don't talk much. I basically say that I feel like I don't have control and that I don't like the feeling. She gives me some suggestions of what to do this weekend since Nick and Charlee will be with their dad.

The ride back home was nice and long. I didn't want to go back home but I promised that we'd finally have chili dogs. The kids made it home safe and I was glad to see them. I know that I love them it doesn't seem like it.

We ate dinner, well I half-way ate. My appetite is gone. I'm trying hard to keep from scratching my face. Well I'll take a melatonin and go to sleep I hope.

October 7th

I'm not sure if I slept, I feel groggy as hell. When I woke I did the stupidest thing, both of my doctor's appointments were yesterday. I rode all the way to Cumberland mall the street way. I was running late and I called the behavioral health and the nurse said "your apt. was yesterday" Luckily I have an apt. for rmonday coming up at 9:30. So I drive back to Atlanta, I go to east Atlanta. I have nervous energy. I don't like that feeling because I'll fly off the handle if someone even looks at me weird. The wings I had were terrible, but the salad and wine were excellent (Flat Iron). I get home at 3:15 and take a nap from 4-4:45.

Something woke me up, but I don't know what. The kids got home, it was raining so hard that I knew they'd be soaking wet. At 7pm we ride up to church for the tent theater, it was 4 hrs but a good time.

11pm, we're home. I'm tired and my head was starting to throb. I've become cranky, thinking negative thoughts.

Does anyone truly care about me? If I just disappeared would anyone give a damn? My whole life has been a lie. How can I teach Nick not to care what others think of him if I struggle with it everyday?

Nick and Charlee need to live with their father. Maybe I should just leave this state. What was wrong with Ellis? Why'd he kill himself? Why do I have children, healthy children? But I feel that they'll turn against me. Will I ever find a mate, someone genuine and caring? What's my purpose here? What have I accomplished? Does my brother Alex ever feel this low? Will I ever be financially stable?

Am I beautiful to anyone? I look so tired my eyes look sunken in. I want to go to sleep. The melatonin and midol are kicking in. I'm very relaxed. It feels good I hope I sleep.

October 8th

I slept great!—with help of course. The payday loan people called. I've paid $200, but I still owe $600 so I'm messed up.

I bought Nick and Charlee breakfast I called aunt L. I told her that C. needs to take them. I'm way way in debt. I owe on everything. I don't know what to do. I came back home and took a nap. We went out to the mall and stayed till 7:30pm. I got Charlee some new shoes, I couldn't find Nick anything but we had a good talk. He said that he's sorry that he doesn't mean to stress me out. I told him that it's best if he learns to stay to himself because he's just like me and people will be jealous of him. I went through it when I was young and I still go through it.

Their father picked them up at 8pm, we met him at the bus station. They were very happy to see him, as always.

I went to a high school classmate's birthday party. It was pathetic. Got home at 2am.

October 9th

I slept off and on. I didn't take anything because it was so late. I got up at 9:30, by the time I got ready for church it was 11:30. I stopped at CVS to get a thankyou card.

Service was interesting. He talked about stress and about what people in the Bible did about it. Afterwards, at the matron's meeting we took pictures of our 75th anniversary.

Ms. T. accosted me in a violent way. She kept asking me for her money back. I tried to move away, she kept walking behind me and was tugging on my coat. I was just about in tears.

I asked sis L. to get her away from me! I left. I skidded out of the parking lot on purpose. I went home, changed clothes, and then went back to the meeting. No one said anything to me. Sis L was speechless. She knows where she went wrong as well as Sis W, V. J, and a few others. I got back home Charles called the kids will be home tomorrow night. I've been in my room relaxing. Ms. T called four times, but each time I heard her voice on the machine I deleted the message. I've taken something to help me sleep.

October 10th

I slept great, with help of course. I got up at 7:50 I'm very nervous about this doctor's appointment. I made it on time, barely, can you believe it. I second guessed myself, passed the exist, got completely turned around. I felt like I was in the Twilight Zone because I was so so so in the area.

Atlanta has these little back streets that lead to nowhere and everywhere. I finally stopped and let out a blood wrenching scream. My throat still hurts. Finally I made it at 9:30 exactly.

The Doctor was so cool, like my other doctor, professional but cool. It was the longest hour of my life. I told her everything and she asked so many questions. God is it 10:30 yet? Finally, the medication I need. She was diligent in explain the positives and negatives. I really appreciate that. That's one of the reasons I always choose female doctors.

I fill the prescription, $5, not bad. Another reason I need to stay with TBS. The ride back to ATL was another Twilight Zone experience. How I ended up in Smyrna is something of a mystery, but finally I75 south toward Atlanta came into view.

Oh God, I'm hungry. I stopped at Publix. I forgot that today is a holiday but the SunTrust branch inside Publix is open. I drove myself to a favorite spot, IHOP on Peachtree—great meal, omlettle, pancakes, four well done sausage links. I did something I've never done I drank the entire pot of coffee and the doctor today told me that I should stay away from caffeinated beverages because caffeine causes anxiety. But I had a taste for coffee.

I'm at another of my favorite spots, East Atlanta Library. I've written a letter to God, I'm also wondering how this medication is going to affect me and I'm not sure how I feel about returning to work. Damn!!! I've said this before, I need to win the lottery. Well I have other things to do I'll write later today.

Well, It's later. I got home at 5:45pm It's good to be gone most of the day. Charlee and Nick will be home at 6pm. As always, Charlee is glad to see me and I her.

C. told me that he's going to talk to me tomorrow. I cleaned the inside of the car it looks great. Then me and the kids rode to McDonalds and also got some car perfume. We're back home, the kids ate in the car. Nick showed me the shoes his dad got him. We're all relaxed now.

I'm looking at my medication wondering about the side effects. I cut them in half and put a week's worth with melatonin in the pill-box and I'll take it.

Ah Yuck Yuck this pill feels like a tiny lump of cement going down and it tastes bad. Well it's going to take two to four weeks for me to feel any effect. God I hope it's a good effect. I'm going to bed now.

October 11th

I didn't really sleep well. I'm apprehensive when it comes to letting something or someone else take control. I can't remember all of what I did today.

Damn!!

October 12th

I didn't sleep too well but I was in a relaxed state. I got up late, 6:30, and I got the kids to the station by 6:45. Back home in bed, I have a doctor's appointment at 3pm.

I left at 2:15. The drive was good and I was sitting on the reversible couch by 3:05. I had a better than usual chat. She asked about work. I told her that I need to go back but I'm trying to switch to a different department. She agreed with that. She asked about male social life, told her I don't have one, she said that's fine as long as its not a prolonged state. She asked if I had a choice in move stars: Matt MaCavahes and Don Cheadle (Matt because of his looks and Don because he seems to have a low key personality).

She asked if I was still confused in what I wanted in a man. I said yes. She told me about a book I should read, I'll pick it up, *Three Goals*, (1) Finances—handle them better, (2) purchasing another home out somewhere, and (3) finding a new job, something without a uniform. She always ends the sessions asking, "Is there anything else on your mind?" I of course say no.

On the way home I take a detour, Piedmont Park, It's so pretty out here. I sit out on a bench and watch people. I think, no bad thoughts, just about life. What I'm doing? What it's for? Why do I feel different than other people, not because of my sickness, but I've always felt different.

I'm home by 5:45, take Nick and Charlee to Little 5 points pizza, they like it. We get home by 8pm, the house is quiet, I take meds by 10pm, I'm relaxed and woosy.

October 13th

I didn't sleep well but was very relaxed, I got up and had the kids at the station by 6:45. I came right back home, no detours, I got in bed, I'm mentally preoccupied with getting prepared to go back to work. I know I can be more. When I finally got up I drove to East Atlanta Library and stayed for 30 min. then I drove to Piedmont Park. It's so beautiful, I don't want to be inside, I want to enjoy this perfect Fall weather. I walked the entire park, looking at the roller bladders and joggers. It's been 2 weeks since I've been to the gym and I feel like it.

I don't want to, but I make my way home thinking about everything and nothing.

October 14th

Slept great, a really deep sleep, didn't even dream. C. called about 9am, she needs to go to GAinsville and check her PO box.

I get dressed and drive Charlee to school by 8:15. I get back and Nicks is getting impatient, the scout master was supposed to pick him up at 9am and now its 9:15. I call the scout master and I ask if we've missed him. He said no. I asked if it'd be better if I bring Nick to church. Before we leave I call D. and ask if she could give Nick some spending money I tell her where he's staying. She has an apartment right across the street from the Washing Plaza dn the Crystal Palace Hostel is right on the plaza. She agrees and suggests that he does a homework assignment for her. She expressed her assignment.

October 26th

As I write these words I feel utterly hopeless. I don't know why. The meds have been in my system for two weeks. My best friend gave me $300 just so I could have money in my pocket. I bought some food and clothes for Nick and Charlee. I'm trying everything: praying, reading the bible, getting outside, thinking positive, trying to be pleasant, trying like hell to hold on to myself.

Help me to understand this madness normal people call "dialing life"? Why can't I tolerate it anymore? I feel cursed like I'm paying for the sins of whoever my parents are. I look at my surroundings I see people that appear to have it all and I know they have stressful times but they are coping, I see the everdya crack heads they even appear to be coping. BUT

THEY ARE UNDER THE INFLUENCE. Well this where my mind is at this point. Hopefully I'll feel better tomorrow.

October 30th

Well tomorrow's the big day after two months of short term disability I return to work. 50% is glad and 50% is scared to death. But I need the money and benefits. I'll be so glad when I can short my acting classes. That's going to be the key to me beginning to feel whole again.

As of this writing I'm at my favorite spot Piedmont Park it's a lovely day, complete blue sky, I see joggers, bikers, Frisbee throwers, dog walkers, just an all around peaceful scene. I'm always so amazed at the 200 year old oak trees out here. If only they could talk.

My morning started off good, for the most part I slept 70% throughout they night. That damn scifi channel has me spoiled. I took a good hot shower, my face is startling clear. I went to breakfast spot the beautiful restaurant. I had an impromptu breakfast with a guy that I've seen every time I eat there. We had great conversation. I drank lots of tea and water. I didn't want it to end. But in my mind I'm saying I've got to enjoy the rest of this day outside. We give each other a hug and part company. While I'm here at the park today I'm going to attempt to run a little, read my bible, and continue to enjoy the scenery.

November 4th

Well since I last wrote, the meds have been in my system 3 weeks. I feel 80% myself. I'm sleeping off and on, my sleeping pattern fluctuates week to week. I've starting work, my classmates were all happy that I came back. I received a lot of hugs. The others just looked at me (but you know what, that's OK). For the most part it felt good to be back. But I'm constantly telling myself nothing has changed. The same morons are still around and they're still morons. I had a doctor's appointment with doctor "All Good". I told her I was feeling much better, got a med refill.

As of this writing I'm at Piedmont Park and I actually ran half mile. It felt great. I have my work cut out for me in regards to getting my physical strength back.

It's amazing I'm starting to realize that I was truly in danger of a complete melt down.

It's such a beautiful day. The sky is tropical in its appearance. The big fluffy white clouds, the air has a warm moisture to it. It's about 75 degrees on a November Atlanta day.

I kind have lot more to do today don't know if I'll get to it through. I need to pay the car note and rent and get my meds filled. Well my children are still with their father. I'm going to attempt to work some overtime Saturday and Sunday. Well that's all for now. I hope to continue to progress positively.

February 21st 2006

It's been three months since I've written. I no longer see doc! I'm going to miss her. Christmas, New Years, and Valentines Day have all passed. I've been abstinent for almost nine months now. It feels great, I did break down and call W. today. He didn't answer (thank God!) so I left him a message telling him I think of him often I thought he would like to hear me say it instead of texting him all the time.

Of course he called back to say that I should call him back, the he misses me, and loves me, and to please call him back.

I got written up today for being tardy. That's three times in 90 days. I was kind of getting depressed but I shook it off. I know I need to get out of this department.

All in all, I still take life day by day. I use my own type of survival skills to make my day at work pass without incident because I absolutely and without a doubt strongly dislike working with black folks, especially when they manage the department.

I've been networking, and gotten some good leads on what departments are hiring at CNN, I just really hope it works out.

I stopped at the store and observed elderly people sometimes my hear goes out to they they look helpless and I start to think about my dad (I had to get a couple of things). And wonder if the younger age group realizes they will get old. And all of a sudden I felt a weird sadness come over me and granted to get a little depressed I shook it off because I realize that I haven't slept in about one week. Hopefully tonight I will. My children are home and I'm glad to see them. I hope I sleep.

April 15th 2006

It's been another two months since I've written a lot has happened, some good, some bad, the percentage varies depending on my mood. I did see W. we made love. I wasn't quite satisfied. I could tell he'd been with someone else. His wasn't as strong as I'm used to. I've haven't seen him since.

I'm convinced now that celibacy is what I want. I feel better then and I feel better now. Without the problems that sex brings wondering where he is, why can't he spend the night, why can't I reach him at certain times.

At this writing of course you know I'm at my favorite place, Piedmont Park, it's about 85 degrees Easter weekend. My mind is cluttered with a lot of things. My dad is very ill. Oh his mind is as strong as ever but physically he's in bad shape, 65 years of drinking straight gin. It's bound to catch up with you.

C. called Dfacs on me. Nick has been living with him now for about 1.5 months. That's a long, long, story.

I got suspended for two days from work, lost the overtime I did and holiday pay. I had enough money to pay rent. A co-worker paid my electric bill. This is most of the bad stuff that's happened the two months I haven't written.

I've started my acting class it's great. I got a call back for an independent film. It felt great to be on a movie set with other actors, some I've worked with before.

June 14th 2006

It's been two months again since I've expressed my thoughts in words. The only personal good thing that's happened for me is W. has been calling quite often. Finally, I called him back of course I did invite him over. We talked for a while, he said that he misses me. No one makes love to him like me. I'm thinking the same about him. He asks me why do I disappear like I do. I tell him because I don't want to get attached. He says as always, "I love you babe" (I refuse to fall for that, I can't afford to—nothing is stable for me now). Anyway, after we talk he kisses me on the lips so passionate and gentle, I melted. Then we talked a little more (I was sitting in my chair. He was kneeling down on the side of the chair. He kissed me again the same way. now I'm thinking this man is dangerous, he knows how to take his time. Of course, you know me I ask him if he wants to get comfortable. He says, "If it's OK with me?" now I had on my green and white short pant pajama set, I believe he knew it was OK. I stand up to help him take his shirt off. This man has the perfect body, I mean perfect, all I could whisper was "you're so beautiful." He was holding and caressing me so damn passionately, damn he's good. I'm staying on my mind. Jazz was playing in the background, the fan was on low. I had my sheer bed curtain draped over the bed candles lit. He picked me up like I was a feather. We were on the bed, he was kissing me like he was deprived of ever kissing a women. I couldn't move and didn't. I enjoyed everything he was doing.

I'm thinking I can't let him have this power over me. I've got to take control of this. Now W. loves to be caressed all over like a women and he loves to be talked to. So of course I take control. But this time it was even. He took it back. Well, I'm thinking I actually need to be controlled right now. So just enjoy it (if I was with a king, but that's another story) I would have called off. I can't begin to explain the way he handled my body, the emotions I was going through. It felt out of this world.

Ok, about the not with a king part. I was terminated because I requested back up about a month ago (May 22nd). My father passed away on May 9th. That has been a devastating blow to me. No one and I mean no one can compare to my daddy. I never saw him harm anyone or anything. The woman he married (R.) has really disappointed me. I now believe she never really cared for my father like he did her. I won't mention her anymore because she's undeserving of it. I haven't been to my acting class in a month. N. C. called me today and asked if I was coming back to class. "Yes" I said.

I've been 50 dollar ringing people to death. My sister isn't talking to me, she did the samething when our mom died (1998). So I guess it will be another four years before we speak eye to eye. My brother moved to Las Vegas. We talked often, but I haven't seen my brother in about six years.

Oh! Once again I'm unemployed! No one knows but my aunt D., she's a God-send. Beautiful, just like my father. If anything happens to her I'm moving back to Arizona. I just can't seem to make it in Atlanta.

My depression has picked up again my medication works on and off. As God as my witness, I don't want anything stronger, I'm afraid of becoming a zombie. I did go to the gym one day, I haven't been in a month, I've lost a lot of muscle tone, not good because I only weigh 110 lbs.

As of this writing, this is how I feel: Like Shit, unworthy, my damn head hurts, I want to give up. My kids, all five of them, are keeping me going. Oh did I mention that Haaj and Elena are expecting children in July and August. I can't help them my car me be repossessed, don't have rent money, the electricity may be turned off. I hate everyone because I feel like everyone hates me, my father's gone. I don't know what to do with myself, I mean damnit I'm 40 years old I have no damn stability. I'm trying so hard to have faith in God I know he's aware of my life. I need Psalm 23 every morning. I pray, I ask "how many times must I go through trials before I am stable? I mean, I really wish I wasn't born. I feel cursed. I mean, I'm serious, I really feel that way. My sleeping pattern is off again.

It's been that way for about 1.5 months, ever since C. called DFACS on me. I haven't quite bounced back. I love my acting class, but I noticed that I'm unable to show emotion when a script calls for it.

I mean I cry alone at night. Oh believe me I feel, I hurt, but I can't express it to anyone but myself or if I'm on the phone with my aunt D—on the phone because she can't see me cry. If I'm going to do this actin thing I've got to show emotion, that's N.C.'s biggest thing with me.

I'm afraid when it happens it's going to be inappropriate. I'm not even going to wish for glup because it probably won't happen.

July 15th 2006

Well it's been a month since I've written, minus 1 day. And as always, a lot has happened. My oldest daughter gave birth to a 7lb 5oz baby boy on 7/7/2006 at 12:47 in the afternoon. His name is Jeremiah Ellison Edwards. I was on the phone while she was giving birth. The father of the baby was also there. I quickly apologized to him because we didn't hit if off well at all. I'm so proud of her. She sent me a picture via my cousin T.'s camera phone. He's a beautiful little guy. I see Ellis all the way. I think Ellis would be very proud to have a grandson. I feel very sad he's not here to be with Elena. El-Haaj has disappeared on me. He did something really stupid. I can only pray this boy doesn't mess up his life. He's too damn intelligent to be fuckin-up like he's doing.

September 20th, 2006

As of this writing at 7:10pm I no longer have my own apartment, my car is about to be legally, if I allow it, reposed. I mean, Nissan and Atlanta, Recovery R is being very nasty with me. The both even sent me text messages. I had lunch with my best male friend Will. It was great to see him. He looks great. He showed me recent pictures of Kayla, she is beautiful. He looks just like his daughter.

I live with N., my best friend's daughter, but Ms. C., my best friend, lives here too. The nice thing about this is that she's allowed me and Charlee to occupy her little boy's room. I pay her $50 per week as long as I'm getting my unemployment.

I'm so off center right now. It was my intent to get here today and read the Bible. You know meditate, but I'm off today and I don't know what caused it.

My sister is having a hard time all of her utilities are disconnected.

September 23rd,

Continuing: I'm here at my favorite spot, Piedmont Park, it's a beautiful Fall day about 83 degrees. While on the way here, I had an epiphany:

What was it you ask—I was in this same mental state last year, on ly I had a fucking job and was receiving a damn paycheck. Now I'm receiving unemployment benefits from the job.

My car needs front breaks so I rode the bus here. It was supposed to rain but it hasn't. I hope tomorrow is as pretty as today.

Anyway, while on the train I thought about my grandmother and I remembered a beautiful Fall day it was windy and chilly probably in the month of October. She wanted to go pick some pecans. I rember we went to the west end, long long long by the train station was there long long long before those apartments were there.

The biggest prettiest pecan tree was right on the corner, full of pecans. She taught me which ones were rotten and which ones were perfect we would crack them when we got back home. They would be so pretty and brown with a nice sweet taste. I really miss her sometimes.

I really hope that I will be able to be a good momzie to Jeremiah and Aushaun.

Sometimes I feel like I haven't been a good parent to any of my children. I don't know if I mentioned the terrible way Elena treated me while I was visiting her

God this is so ironic. I'm in the same place as last year except this tie I forgot to mention on the previous page I have really no medical insurance. I get food stamps, I live with my friend's daughter, and I'm trying my damnedest to keep me an Charlee the hell out of her way. you know people treat you like shit when they know you have nothing.

Point blank, I've got to get out of this Sodom and Gomorra city. It's beautiful and all I know some beautiful places to go but why the hell can't I make it here. I mean shit Ah fuck it, I don't care anymore.

And you know, what else I don't even know who I am. I mean when you don't even know who your parents are and it seems like you hatched out of a damn egg in a forest. Damn-it, it is enough to work on your psyche.

Somebody in this family I was adopted into has to know something. This is just the way I'm feeling right now. Pretty much all the damn time I feel like this, some days it's worse than others.

It's a debilitating state of mind. It's really really really really messing with me.

You know what I tried to do today. I tried to pawn my gold rings. Why the hell would you need an ID if you're trying to pawn your own shirt?

I'm trying to figure out how to get marta cards for me and Charlee next week. The rings don't mean much anyway, I mean I bought them and that's what jewelry is for, emergencies like these (Will taught me that).

Charles has really stooped to another low. He's stopped paying child support. I told him I was moving. He wants Charlee (no way) so he's thinking I'm going to take him to court and he's going to say this about me: she tried to kill herself, she picked up and left her oldest three children, she can't keep a job, she doesn't have a place to say (black men and be so cruel) Déjà vu all over again.

This beautiful city has really turned sour.

November 26, 2006:

It's 2:30 pm. I've found a nice relaxing spot down the street from my favorite park. I'm trying desperately to acquire a taste for latte's but I'm too embarrassed to ask for extra sugar. When I arrived at the park it was so beautiful. 70 degrees and leaves of all colors were falling; red, green, orange, and brown. Even though I don't like cold weather, there's something so beautiful and innocent about falling leaves and how they smell.

November 30, 2006

Boy was I sluggish this morning. It was very warm last night, so I was sweating in my sleep. Not to mention I was a little shell-shocked from all the bumping that took place Tuesday night upstairs in my sisters house. I'll tell you about that later.

Anyway, hell week at the gym has been just that. My legs are sore as hell. Sharon, the instructor, is awesome. Right now I'm at IHOP on Peachtree. I'm trying to get my diet balanced now that I'm back in the gym and somewhat on a regular basis. Anyway, I had the new pancake combo. I ate every bit of it.

As of right now in Atlanta, the weather is absolutely beautiful. It's been 70 degrees ever since Thanksgiving. The mornings have started off very cloudy and gloomy but by noon nothing but sunshine, blue sky, and a warm breeze finishing off the last of the falling leaves.

I was offered a job yesterday as a security supervisor at Suntrust Plaza Headquarters right in the heart of downtown. I hope my intelligence is not insulted by being offered a demeaning salary. Women are often insulted that way. That's why I haven't gotten too excited yet.

I'm getting sleepy as hell right now. My thoughts are beginning to jump around in my head.

December 26, 2006:

It's been exactly one month since I've written. The things I have to tell you will blow your mind. But first, some very good news. I have a damn job! As a supervisor! I know! Can you believe it? I started December 11th. So far I love it. It's a challenge, something I thrive on. My boss is great! Very fair. My first paycheck will come on December 29th so when I tell you I'm strung out until Friday, I'm strung out until Friday. I looked at a one bed-room apartment for $485.00 a month. The lady I talked to said it's really nice. I told her I would love to move in by January first or the 11th at the latest. I'll meet her this Saturday at 2 pm There's no deposit and no application fee but there is a $150.00 administration fee that is non-refundable which I thought was funny. The weather is cold and gloomy. But I'm at work and right now Charlee is with her Dad for the Holiday. I miss her when she's not with me.

She and I have been through a lot together. I only hope this makes her a strong woman. My boy Nick has been through a lot too. I hope he's been learning what kind of man he should be by looking at how much of a dumb-ass his father is. What a total disappointment C has turned out to be. Anyway, those were quick thoughts that needed to be released.

You know, I used to hear my mother say blood is thicker than water and I never knew what that meant, but she always said it. In terms of family and non-family. An example (momma's baby-daddy maybe) meaning momma's going to always treat the baby right because she carried it in her womb and gave birth; but daddy's not sure about baby so he's gonna treat baby with a long-handled spoon because maybe baby's not his and doesn't deserve to be treated like his. Anyway, I know what I'm trying to say. It will come together as I continue to write.

January 15, 2007:

I'm wide awake, and my cycle is on. I'm jittery. There's so much I need to catch up on, writing wise. Well, I'm too preoccupied with something subconsciously. I can't seem to relax. It's now 1:47 in the morning so I'm going to stop at this point until I can relax and think clearer.

January 21, 2007:

okay, now that I've had sex maybe I can think straight. Let's see . . . where do I start. Oh yeah! I need to tell you about that situation at my sisters house. Every night I try to lay down at about 8:30-9:00 pm After I take my medication so I can go to bed. I do remember falling asleep and then waking up because I was sweating. As I was getting comfortable, my sisters house, as usual, was wide the fuck open. It was about 11:30 pm And every thug in the neighborhood was in her house. Music was loud, E was at work. Her baby K and S's baby (I can never remember her name) were also wide awake. I believe Charlee was with her Dad. Anyway, I dropped off into a deep sleep and all of a sudden, I heard running up and down my sisters hallway. Doors were slamming, loud thuds against the wall and strange men and woman's voices. Then I heard A, my sisters daughter say "y'all need to stop". Then I heard thunderous thuds against a wall. I was scared as hell. I didn't know who the hell was in my sisters house. I was praying that they didn't come downstairs where I was. I grabbed my phone, called my sister. I was shocked as hell. She answered the phone. I will finish this story later. I have gotten too tired.

February 9, 2007:

I had a great week at work. It's Friday I'm home. But for some odd reason I need the lights on. It feels comfortable tonight. I had to ask God for forgiveness tonight. C pushed me to a point where if he walked in front of me and I had any kind of weapon, I would have killed him. I absolutely hate this man.

I called his sister, L, and we talked. And it was no holes barred. I told her exactly how I feel about C. I'm tired of fighting people. My kindness is being taken for weakness. I'm so drained right now. All kinds of thoughts are running through my mind.

Like what the hell is my purpose. When will I feel sane, who the hell am I. Will I find a mate that will accept me for all of my ups and downs? When will I feel complete, whatever complete is. I mean, I really like my job, I feel challenged. The company acknowledges me as an asset. But every now and then, I feel lost as hell. When it comes to my personal life, I still feel alienated from my oldest three children. I'm just not sure how to get over that feeling. I do however know that I have no family here in Atlanta. Everyone has shown me that. I will write about that another time.

My brother has been my rock for a long time now. I wish he was here. I think he and I could accomplish a lot together.

February 11, 2007:

I have been tossing and turning all night long. My mind is beyond cluttered. Fuck! I'm miserable. My skin is itching. All kinds of thoughts are going through my mind. I have a very difficult decision to make. What the hell am I going to do about Nick? What, what, what, what? Why am I going through this dejavu? C is doing exactly what E did to me. He's trying to take my children. I need to sever all ties with C, but to do that, I've also got to sever all ties with Nick. I need to do this for my fucking sanity. C is starting to occupy negative space in my mind. But because we have children together, unfortunately, he must live only because his children love him. I personally want the bitch dead.

Why, God, does it seem that when people do wrong to other people, and they know they are doing wrong, why do they sleep at night with no problem? Why do they act as thought they've done nothing wrong? And they know they have. Why must the poor unsuspecting victim of their wrong do the suffering? Why, God, must I continue to absorb pain? Emotional pain. Don't you know I'm tired? I'm tortured not knowing when people are going to stop hurting me.

I wish my brother was here to take care of me. I really would like to try his organic diet. I feel it. Maybe when all these things are out of my system. I'll fall asleep. It's times like this when I'm glad I work the 3-11 shift.

I miss Charlee when she's gone. I think she misses me too. It's Sunday morning by the way and I wanted to go to church. I need to be in the house of the Lord, but I'm afraid of the church folk. My neighbor was real sweet and fixed some collards and cornbread. My food stamps came this month. And hopefully today I'll have a tax refund check. I'm starting to relax and that's good. Maybe I'll drift off to sleep. I will be so glad when the weather starts to warm up so I can exercise. Damn! I miss having a vehicle. I miss the freedom of just getting lost on some highway and trying new restaurants. I'm hungry. Damn!

February 17, 2007:

It's 4:13 pm on a cold Saturday afternoon. My morning was outstanding. My old flame W finally broke me down. You know I have to give him credit. He's very persistent Anyway, he has been calling on a regular basis for quite some time. On Valentines Day I texted him and you know what he did? He called me from his new cell phone number. Told me to answer. And as always, when I don't recognize a number, I answer "This is Mrs. Fernanders". He said "It's me girl!" I was glad to hear his voice. My body immediately began to melt. I visualized him naked in front of me. My panties got wet. My nipples got hard. I started throbbing. We had small talk for a quick minute. Don't even expect for me to remember what we talked about. We both acknowledged that we missed each other. My voice went from professional, because I was at work, to soft and sensuous. Then I said I want you to spend the night with me tonight. He said "oh, how about we spend Saturday morning together?" I said ok and he responded with "Early early Saturday!", and I said "okay". I couldn't sleep worth a damn. I was so excited.

He arrived at 8:30 am before that, I took a long hot bath and maintenanced my body real good. I put on my red camisole and black panties with a tiny red design. I turned the radio to my favorite jazz station. Damn, he looks and smells good. Now, if I may give myself credit, W is the only man that I know for a fact that I have turned completely on.

Now of course it didn't take long for us to become naked. We examined each other all over. Smelling, touching, kissing and caressing. His hands felt great. His fingers felt even better. I was losing my mind. I love the way he plays with my hair. He loves to see my hair fall in my face when I'm on top straddling him. He looks at me and says softly, "sexy, sexy". By this time, I've broken a slight sweat. Now mind you, it's 33 degrees outside and I have the window cracked open because I know how we get down, so the cold breeze that softly blew in felt good. I'm thinking "Oh God, he hasn't even entered me yet and I'm about to explode". He kisses me real passionate and hard. I'm trying so hard not to beg him to penetrate. Finally, softly I say, "I'm ready for you to cum inside me". How else can a woman describe a man that fits perfectly into her? But oh god! I stroke him a couple of times, then I stop and move off of him because I don't want to cum that fast. I tell him that. Then, I take my time and kiss him all over and everywhere. I love the slightest touch with my tongue on him makes him grab the sheets with his fist. That is so damn erotic. I continue to kiss, rub, and stroke him all over his beautiful black muscular body. He tells me to come to him. He wants to see me while he taste me. Like is aid, I maintenanced my body real real good. Ohhh his tongue, the way he's sucking me. "Stop!", I say. I'm about to explode. He puts himself inside me and tells me to sit on him all the way. Ah! Damn! Damn this is just too good.

I'm trying to not cum. I aggressively start stroking him. I feel it! I feel it! I feel it! Oh God yes! I start to cry and I kiss him aggressive and hard so he can't tell (hopefully) that he's just fucking me up. My body is soaking wet. I'm shivering, not from the window being open though. He holds me. "It's okay", he says. I whisper to him "What is it that you do to me?". And I don't know about him, but I fall sleep.

I feel myself get cold and he pulls the covers over us. Jazz is playing in the background. Damn, this feels good. He falls asleep. He recovers quite nicely. He rolls over on top of me, opens my legs with his legs and enters me; strokes me so damn hard and good. I'm speaking a foreign language. In my mind, I'm thinking this is what I need. I tell him to take me, that I'm his. He strokes me harder and harder. I'm losing my mind right about now. But I'm holding him close to me. I don't want him to stop. Again, the feeling a woman gets when the fit is perfect is unspeakable. I feel him get harder and harder and I'm getting hotter and hotter and wetter and wetter and at the same time we both reach Mount Everest. He shivers on top of me like he's in a freezer. All I could do was lay there and hold him on top of me. We doze off for a quick minute, look at some television. He has to go and I'm hungry as hell. I take a wash off. I want his smell to linger on me. Then he drops me off at my favorite restaurant. He gives me a kiss. We do, however, have a great political conversation on the way there. What a great morning.

May 6, 2007

I've had a bad couple of weeks. Needless to say, when that happens my skin breaks out like I have the plague. It all started when I told N and the baby that she could come and stay with me because she and her mothers husband were not getting along. N and the baby arrived at about 11 pm on a Sunday night. I was tired and had not been sleeping. I was not looking forward to going to work on Monday. But I was excited to have her and the baby stay with me. We caught a cab from the Greyhound Bus Station. A (the baby) was wide awake; smiling and playing and maybe a little nervous. I mean, he had never been to my home. So I told N that they could sleep in my bed. She took a shower and I went to the living room and tossed and turned all night. First thing I thought was that I've got to get another bed and more food and that I hoped she could help with Charlene's hair and homework. Now those last two thoughts are totally my selfish way of thinking that other people think like I do. When will I learn that they don't? Anyway, after a week or less, A had started crawling to me and allowing me to hold him. I did notice that he cries a lot and it seemed like all the time. That was nerve-wracking.

A little after a week had passed and Charlee had a half day of school, she arrived home at about 1:30 in the afternoon. I had just enough time to let Charlee know about some boy she was going to sneak and see, but that also I was glad she came home.

Anyway, at about 6:45 pm I got a call from Charlee talking about some lady that said she knows me and was trying to fight N. I asked Charlee where N and the baby were. She said everybody is in the house. I said ok and told them to stay there. I heard N in the background saying "No, don't come home. Everything is okay!". I hung up the phone.

Less than 5 minutes later, Charlee calls me crying and just about hysterical. The lady threw a brick through the living room window. When I arrived home, N was bleeding on her hand and had already called the police. She also sustained a very nasty human bite on her right breast. Glass was all over my fucking floor and the window was knocked completely out of the frame. The brick was in the spot it landed after coming through the window. About 15 ft. in the corner. I was a hot mothafucka. I wanted to kick N's ass because of the story she gave behind the whole incident. Totally avoidable! Totally!

Once again, my whole self was thrown off balance. I was now nervous as hell to leave N at my home. She had been talking to Ms. P. Ms. P had picked her up at my house several times already. My balance was completely gone now.

May 28, 2007:

I always start off with the same old line, "It's been a while since I've written". But instead of starting off on a negative, it's a fun beginning to this chapter and possibly a start to a new relationship. I went to the Atlanta Jazz Festival Saturday. I got there about 4 pm and ran into a coworker. We had a great time and met a guy whom was already there. You know whats bad about this part is that I can't remember his name for shit. Anyway, an older gentleman. He had a long beard, eye glasses, receding hairline, and his hair was curly. He had clean white teeth and clean hands. Anyway, we ended up staying at the festival Saturday until Herbie Hancock played. He walked us to the midtown train station. We all agreed to attend Sunday also.

I arrived at 5:30 and K was already there. I spotted her right off because we all agreed to sit as close to the same spot as possible, which was damn near the front row of the main stage. Just as I spread my blanket out, I looked up and there he was. I gave him a hug. His eyes lit up. I could see it through his daytime goggles as he calls his shaded eyeglasses. He said I looked everywhere for you guys. I didn't think you were going to make It. I have seats for us closer than yesterday. Come on, he cheerfully said. While we were walking to our spot, K said she would be leaving after Purim performed, which was an outstanding performance. He asked me if I would be going also. Oh no, I'll be here, I said. In my mind I'm thinking, there's no way I am going to miss Pete Escavedo and Sheila E perform. When K left, she gave me her C.D. She's also a musician.

We placed our chairs close to each other and enjoyed Mr. Hutcherson and his quartet which was very romantic, touching, and fun. The lady playing the piano in this group was the best I'd heard during the day. She was the coolest piano player I've ever seen. She received a standing ovation when introduced. While the Hutcherson Quartet played, we talked to each other about personal things. We became a little more comfortable and he said I bought you something yesterday. He went on to explain that he likes to support the Jazz Festival and to keep it free, he purchased me a T-shirt. I was so flattered. I mean, it was a simple gesture and to me it mean that he found something about me appealing. It's been so so so long since a man has shown a romantic interest. And it's been so so so long since I've actually felt intellectually interested in a person. This man makes me want to do better when it comes to my appearance. I mean, by no means am I unattractive, but I haven't been a lady in a very very long time. I haven't worn make-up or worn my naturally long hair down like I used to.

Anyway, after the quartet, we walked around a bit and he bought me something to eat. We talked some more. I saw Sergeant W (she looked great). When we got back to our seats, Pete Escavedo was all set up and ready to go. Sheila E looked like a queen. It was the most high energy performance. It was perfect. That damn girl put an ass whippin on those drums. Her dad was so cool and very well dressed. He didn't even break a sweat. We had the best seats and we danced and sang along. She drummed to some of Prince's old songs from purple rain. We started packing our things and headed out the park. The crowd was immense and a hell of a lot more than Saturday's crowd.

On the way to the station (Midtown), I held his arm and he changed it to holding my hand. He told me more about himself. He's a write. He's written three novels and two on the way. He has one son that is 19 years old. He works at Georgia State University (I still can't think of his name) and is looking forward to a good retirement. He told me how his mother died of cancer a couple of years ago and she lived with him, but he had to put her in a hospice. But she gave him the re-awakened strength to start writing. When we got to the train station, I stopped to look for my MARTA card and then, he said I want to give you another hug. And I looked at him and saw how sensitive he is, and that he looked at me as though to say don't play with my feelings. I thought about him as I walked home. And how I would not play with his person's feelings. He is a genuine person, a good person. And I feel like he would be able to make me a better person. I was just about home and he called me and asked me my favorite color. "Blue", I said and he said "i just sculpted you a horse and it looks funny, but I was thinking about you. And you're favorite animal is a horse. The next time I see you, I'll give it to you." We talked about Charlee and how he wants to meet her. He's invited us to the symphony this Saturday. I also liked that about him because he immediately included my children.

July 16, 2007:

I'm going to tell you a lot of things. But it's going to begin in a backwards sort of way. I'm feeling a lot of dejavu lately. How can I explain myself? Well, I guess I can put it this way. I want a house with a garden. A long long ways away. I want my two youngest children to have what I tired to give them quite some time ago when I had my house on Alvarado Terrace; their own room with decent furniture. I'm almost positive that's why Charlee doesn't like coming home. I mean, this is a great huge apartment with a lot of potential. But I can't quite get comfortable here. I don't know what it is. Maybe it's my work schedule. Maybe it's me again. I'm not nearly as disturbed as I was last year at this exact time. I mean, I was literally homeless. But this year is a different hurt and pain. I'm losing my 12 year old daughter. She doesn't like to be around me. I'm positive that a lot of this stems from last year. I've got to somehow get her back on a schedule. I need a job and I don't foresee my work hours changing anytime soon. And I keep telling myself thank God for this job. I learned last year the very very very very and very hard way that people really do kick you when you're down.

My dad's house and my grandmothers house had gardens and a beautiful smell. I can't seem to get that here. Maybe the carpet in the two rooms here is bothering me. It was here when I moved in and I had it cleaned before I moved my bed in and before I allowed Charlee to sleep in her room. I need to have it cleaned again. I absolutely hate my crackhead neighbors. However, I am blessed that they have not robbed me. That could be because one of the biggest crackheads, there is a guy I literally have known since I was in 4th grade. I don't think any of them work. At least nothing steady.

July 17, 2007:

Well, I became really tired last night and very uneasy while writing, so let me see if I can finish my thoughts. D, the man I met at the Jazz Festival, well he freaked out on me. I mean, we're still boyfriend and girlfriend or fiance. Sunday morning, well Saturday afternoon, me and D walked to the store where he lives. I asked him if I could have some turkey bacon for breakfast on Sunday. I noticed he hesitated with an answer but then he said "anything you want". I asked if he was sure.

Later that night, we went to a movie. Okay, I was good with everything but he was extremely tired. I really wasn't in the mood for love-making because I wanted him to rest. I could tell something was on his mind.

Anyway, the next day he came to my job and he told me that he thinks that he's lost me because of sharing what he was thinking and what he was thinking was this. With our two incomes, he was basically going to continue to take care of the bills at the house that his ex-wife lives in. so I wrote him a 4 page letter explaining to him that there's no way he could take care of two households. And in so many words, in which I did not come out and say, there was no way in hell I was going to use my income for him to continue to take care of his ex-wife. But I told him if C, his son, needs anything that I would not hesitate. And that he gave her everything; cars, the house, the land, and all for one damn dollar. I commended him on being on hell of a man for doing that. So he wrote me a letter sayin he didn't know that I didn't like him. I mean basically, he ignored the rest of the letter. I also said in the letter that we needed to slow it down a whole lot and we should keep both places. But that part I told him in person. Also in the letter he wrote to me, he sent me a book of quotes and the quotes are basically saying I judged him.

Basically, I don't know anymore how I feel about him. I mean, Lord knows with two incomes, both of us can do a lot. But I see a big problem in which he is not going to address. He always praises himself. Oh I try so hard, and D paid for your acting lessons and I'm a good man. At first I thought he was doing that to impress me, but that's something he does all the damn time. And I know me. I will get tired of hearing and say something that will really hurt his feelings. So this weekend I haven't talked to him at all. I did call when I was at Ms. H's house, but he didn't answer and I didn't call again.

July 31, 2007:

Well, it's the last day of July. Me and D have been together now for almost 3 months. I'm very glad we're not married. I'm also glad that we didn't get his mothers ring sized. And I believe he feels the same way. I have ways that will never understand. And he has ways that in the long run will get to me.

He did something that really pissed me off. After acting class Saturday, a group of us always get together. He joined in and basically took over the conversation. I did not like that at all. I can see that as much as I need an extra income, I'd rather do this on my own. I love him dearly, but he, I believe, will become quite possessive. And I cannot be possessed. Remember, I had that same issue with C.J. I couldn't stand it. Anyway, I ended up spending all of last week with D.

The good thing about it was my apartment was not bothered. So my crackhead neighbors, whom I all know, actually respect my wishes of not robbing me. As of this writing, I'm sitting on the screened in porch. I don't know if I've ever described my place, but it's nice. Oh yeah, I think I have. Well, the porch has a lot of potential also. I wish I had my wind chimes. This morning would be perfect to hear their soft ringing.

D has been with me at my place since Sunday evening. It's Tuesday and I can't tolerate him anymore. It feels so good to have this alone time in my place. It's clean. I've eaten and I'm listening to my 97.5 music station and I just feel relaxed. I do miss my two little children terribly so. They're growing up and I've got to realize that. Nick is so sweet. Both he and Charlee always tell me they love me. I am a bit worried about having D in my life when it comes to Charlee because she's so much like her father. I get anxious that she will hurt D's feelings and he will hurt hers. And my children will forever be first in my life, especially my two young ones. I miss them so much.

They're father really disrupted our life. I am so trying to forgive him but sometimes I feel so much hatred for him. I can visualize torturing him so he can feel the hurt he's caused to his two children and me. Nick is very easy-going. Charlee, I'm so afraid she's picked up on the depression gene I carry. I've got to really watch her. Her cycle started Saturday night. I wanted so much to be with her when it happened. She made me feel so proud. She called and left me a message. And then Sunday night when we finally talked, she told me all about it. How it happened. She wasn't scared. That she kind of knew what it was. She remembers that I've been talking to her about this since she was ten years old.

Anyway, back to the D issue. I'm going to call him at his office and let him know that I'm going to spend the rest of the week by myself. Oh God, I already know the biggest question he'll ask. "Am I crowding you? Have I done something wrong?" I've got to get him to realize that every time we're together, he doesn't have to be all over me. Sexually, now I will say that I do have great orgasms. But I am starting to hate the fact that he can't always use his penis and I prefer that after he kisses me all over. Sometimes, I'm giving him little hints about that.

Anyway, there are benefits to this relationship. Both of our leases are up in March and April. We have much more to learn about each other. Oh yeah, he asked for a key to my apartment. For right now that is going to be a negative. I do not want to come home and see this man every night right now. I've got to also get myself back in a more realistic schedule. I've got to get back into the gym. I mean, don't get me wrong, D has awakened me. He's making me feel like a woman; loved, worthy, important. He respects me. But I've got to make him feel the same way and he is all of those things.

I've been on my own for 14.5 years. I've gone from living in a homeless shelter and under a house for two days to the top of my game. And now this man literally from nowhere has come full speed ahead into me and my children's lives. Yeah, we need to keep both apartments. It's too much that we still need to know about each other. And we've never talked about how much financial help he's giving his ex-wife. The financial thing is going to be a big issue and I'm not going to have a joint account with him like I was thinking. I make way too much money compared to his income.

And again, how much financial support is he giving to his ex-wife? He has not mentioned it since I wrote him that letter.

September 10, 2007:

Didn't know it was going to be so long before writing again. Anyway, D pissed me off so bad Friday night. I could have really really gotten nasty with him. As of right now, I can't see myself marrying him. He has a lot of issues. But it's one thing I can say he told me about how he's used to getting his way. How he can be very manipulative. And that he can't seem to be that way with me. Number one, because it's not working and number two, because he claims he just can't. I told him that I've seen his manipulative ways and for 30 years, his wife J put up with a lot of shit. But I refuse to. I also told him that I know also for 30 years that he's been used to 2 incomes. But right now, as I see it, we will for a long long time be engaged.

So later that night, well let me start first when we had wine and cheese. It's always romantic and we have a beautiful romantic night. So this night was beautiful. But he did something that repulsed me so bad. This man started whimpering like a baby, and then he literally started crying. I could have slapped the crap out of him. And then, he said "Menashaa". It was different tonight. Crying, I could have slapped him. Oh that was so fuckin weak. He looked sickening. He made my stomach turn. I didn't want him to touch me at all for the rest of the weekend.

Class was great Saturday and the play I saw my acting instructor in was great. We had a great time. When we got home, I wanted a cup of warm tea and I immediately went to bed. I couldn't bare for him to touch me. It's kind of funny. He's trying everything in his power to get me to be under one roof. I really think he's more interested in having two incomes so he can help his wife and son. Because again, we've never discussed my letter that I wrote him. Anyway, Sunday morning I came home. I really enjoyed my quiet time but I miss Charlee.

The next time D pulls that crying shit on me, I have a real surprise for him.

October 1, 2007:

Well, I got married on September 21, 2007. had a great ceremony. Had a great honeymoon. My memories and pictures will tell a great story. And soon I will write down all of the details. But until then, other things are on my mind. Okay, C.J. Always told me tat he had never met anyone like me, I was different. Yeah, whatever. Well, it seems that D is the same way. Only I see it as a sick obsession. I still can't understand why he wants to spend every waking minute with me. I mean literally, a few minutes ago, he was so damn sleepy and tired that his eyes were crossing. To me, he's being possessive. Maybe I just don't know. How, I mean how do I explain this? No one should want to be with a person every waking moment of the damn day. I mean, he told me "I missed you so much today". I thought about D today. I really did. But damn, not like he thought about me. This man is going to fuckin smother me. I don't know how else to express to him not to fucking do that. It's actually a turn off. As much as I want to make love to him tonight, he just will not let me warm up to him. And then he goes into this "i didn't mean to overwhelm you." I mean, we had a great conversation. I'm glad him and Charlee had a great day because I was worried about that. But give me some space. Stop being all over me. I mean shit! It's not that damn deep for me. Well, that's enough of that. I have been doing well in my acting class. I feel as though I'm a lot better than the first time I started acting class. But I will talk about that another time.

October 10, 2007:

Wednesday at D's apartment. I'm doing something that I rarely do. I've taken my journal out and I'm quickly writing my thoughts down because I'm feeling caged like I need to get away from D. But if I write, maybe these thoughts will go away. I have 1.5 months to enjoy my apartment on my own. I've got to get some time to myself.

October 21, 2007:

Well, since I've written last, D is still smothering me. Charlee acts like she hates D. I really can't seem to talk to her anymore. She's really trying his patience and mine. She has really put him in some bad situations. Especially when he's picking her up from my job and she leaves my view.

Last Monday it was bad what she did at the West-end train station. She really could have D put in jail.

Well, to add a footnote about having the apartment 1.5 months, Thank God, I had an epiphany and I wrote D a note and asked him to tell his apartment managers that he will not be breaking his lease. His lease is up next May. I was so glad to hear that because he needs to really learn how I am. I think I need next week, or part of it, just me and Charlee. To tell you the truth, they are both getting on my damn nerves. D because he's trying to kiss Charlene's ass and I asked him not to do that.

November 2, 2007:

I've had some nice quality time to myself this week. I've been doing a lot of reflecting. Reflecting about my grandmother, my dad, El-Haaj and N and more and more often about E. When I think about my grandmother, it's always how she was very protective of me. The good times I had when I would visit every weekend up until she moved in with us. When I was in the 8th grade. Our relationship was never the same when she moved in on Beecher Street. When I think about my dad, it's how sweet he was to my mother. He seemed to never have any harsh words towards her. How he bent over backwards to help me and my sister when my mom passed away. I used to think I never had anyone there for me. No one to call on when I needed something. But my father was always there up until he was forced to die. Why am I only now realizing how much he loved me? Maybe all this reflection is a sign that I'm aging. You know, getting old . . . it scares me, because I don't know if it's a good sign. I think about N because I really hate the way I had to speak to her. It really tugs at my heart when I remember how A knew something wasn't right after me and his mom argued. He was so confused and to pick up on something at such an early age. I think about El-Haaj because I know what it's like to love someone so deeply and not have them understand how special they are.

And E, why have I been thinking about him? It is a mystery to me. It seems as though every place in Atlanta I've been going lately, we had gone there. I took a walk in Piedmont Park and he was so heavy on my mind it was scary. Maybe he's watching over me. Him and my Dad. And last but not least, D . . . it gets easy sometimes and it gets hard sometimes. Day by day I have to tell myself that I will write at another time. The funny situation that is happening right before my eyes.

November 23, 2007:

I had a very pleasant surprise Sunday. I called my son El-Haaj. Well he called me first about two days before and left me a very strange message. No need for me to write it down. I'll always remember what he said. Anyway, we had a nice conversation. He asked me some things about his dad and I had to tell him his dad wasn't very nice to me. Basically because he could not control me. And I told him I know that's whats going on with him and N and he agreed. Anyway, I made sure to tell him I loved him and that he is very special to me. I've also been going through regrets about marrying D. It's not right. Damn! I don't even know if I love him. Hell, did I ever love him?

I remember my friend W asked me if I loved him or just what he does to me (sexually). I was sure then and sure now that I actually loved W.

I'm starting to believe that I love what D does to me sexually. I've always wanted someone to be totally uninhibited. I really really really really and really enjoy how he seems to worship my body when he's making love to me. He prefers to be in control when we are in that way. All my other lovers preferred for me to be dominate over them.

I've been needing to write for a long time now. When my mind is cluttered, I've noticed it's because I haven't written. This helps me so much. Also, the day of Thanksgiving I was very depressed. I really don't like a lot of my quasi-relatives on my Dad's side. They are the most ghetto people. I've never felt comfortable around them. Even at the family reunions. Ever since I've been an adult. That is because they all know I'm not family. Now I absolutely love my Aunt D and Aunt S but she kinda looks at me strange. My Uncle A., he looked so much like my dad yesterday. I even heard my dad's voice sound of his voice. The sound of his voice filled me with joy. My Aunt G., I really care for all of these people. But those other ones that I care not to name, I could really give a damn if I ever saw them again.

As I write these lines, I want to run so far away. Nick and Charlee keep me from losing my damn mind. People really don't understand what a struggle my mind puts me through. D is no help. He's a control freak and weak as hell. I find myself having to rethink my feelings for him. The agony I'm feeling of what I've done (marriage) is really playing with my mind. I thought he was more cultured than he is. Now, he reads a lot of books, but he's not cultured. E was cultured. I would even say W is more cultured. I know I'm more cultured than he is. I think it's because I know when to shut up.

I wrote D a letter in the summer basically expressing my thoughts on hoping we weren't just having a summer romance. Well, I think that's what it was. A very passionate, awakening experience for both of us. Him because of his wife (and this is what he told me) was in menopause and was not loving him. They had basically been living in separate areas at the house for 10 years. I mean this man is so open and explicit sexually that it's great for me. And I believe he's always wanted to express that talent. He says so every time we make love. For me, I've had great lovers. Hell,

I'm a great lover, so really he can't turn me out. He is, however, turning me off because he basically lied about his finances. And right now, in my life, at my age, I need financial security and that means someone who is not depending on my income along with theirs to be secure. They have to already have their shit together and I thought he did. So now, the great conundrum is how do I deal with this?

I'll pray for patience. Another thing that bothers me, and this is something my brother brought to my attention, I had a lot to do with my termination at CNN. I should have not said anything when M moved me to another post. I would probably have the same work hours, hence having time like I sued to with Nick and Charlee. The other thing I still hate is what C did with the Dfacs thing. That was the icing on the rotting cake. He tore us apart. Sometimes, it feels like forever . . . me, Nick and Charlee. All I wanted him to do was give Nick male guidance. And like a bitch, shit that a scored woman would do, he called Dfacs. I want so much to have my family back. I need that stability.

Charlee is still not as stable as she would like to be. I've got to get her a real bed. Every chance she gets, she wants to be at Ms. H's house. She has expressed to me more than twice how she misses Nick. And how we used to do things. The walks we took after dinner, how we used to look at television together in my room. To write about this makes me want to cry, but D is sitting right in front of me and it's only 8:15 pm. Dark as shit outside. He doesn't have a TV. Shit! Shit! Shit! Shit! I miss how It used to be.

I love my job. It's something I have always wanted. A supervisor position. It's the fucking hours. D asked me what it would take for me to get daytime hours. I told him someone would have to die. And that's true. I work for a great company.

I miss Charlee and she misses me too. She worries about me and I'm starting to see that. It's glad to know she cares. Nick, he's a confused little boy at age 14. I had a really good talk with him and told him it's basically time for him to get it together and take the blame for the decisions that he's making. I had the same talk with Charlee. I just feel like something has got to give. I still don't have my stability back. I've got a job, benefits, a landlord that's working with me, but no real stability. And I am thinking about E more and more. What is he trying to tell me. I miss my sister and brother and my dad something terrible. I wonder if we, my sister and brother, will ever see each other again. There are no more quasi-family members funerals that can bring us together. My dad was the only one left. What am I to do now with myself? This marriage isn't going to work, I'm afraid. I feel it. Well at least we don't want children. All I can do is pray. I wonder if we're going to have wine and cheese. Is he going to want to make love to me? Is it going to feel great like always? What feelings do I really have for this man? Why in the hell did I get married? Why? I must pray, I must pray, I must pray, and I must pray.

December 5, 2007:

There are so many thoughts going through my soul right now. I am the most miserable person around. I've been totally withdrawn at work on purpose. I haven't combed my hair in a couple of days on purpose. Damn it, I just don't feel like it. I am so disappointed in D. he turned out to be broke as hell. Shit! He can't help me with shit! I'm helping him more than he's helped me financially. It's over! We are no longer married. Two months, exactly. The courtship, however, was beautiful. It ended up being exactly what I thought a summer romance should be. We ruined it. By marrying. He's weak and it makes me sick to look at him. He cries at the drop of a hat. That is the ugliest thing a man can do in front of me. With the exception of losing a loved one. I've come to the conclusion that I don't know what true love is. To be in love . . . i really don't know what it feels like. I need a strong man. I've been involved with two men that fit that category of a strong man, that kept me in check. W and W.

D talked for a very long time on the phone earlier this week. And I told him that I don't know what it's like to really love someone unconditionally, with the exception of my children. But I've never loved a man that way. I told him that I was very sorry that I've hurt him by being so cold when I'm getting points and opinions across to him. With him, it's the only way I know how to be. Because if he's so damned emotional then one of us has to be the strong one. Dare I say the man! Well, fuck! I'm the woman! I've told him several times that because of the job I have, I basically have to be a man at work. And I don't want to come home and play the man role too. Sometimes, he would just come over to me and lay his head on my shoulder so damn submissive and weak that I wanted to slap the shit out of him. It was so weak and feminine. I mean something a woman would do. Well, anyway, I got my key back to the small master lock. I no longer want to go inside of his apartment and I don't want him at mine. We both have a couple of things at each others place though. I'm writing these lines in the hopes that I will feel a little bit better emotionally. But I, again, am finding myself struggling during the Holiday's and fucking broke . . . again. As it has been a while since I can remember in my adult life. I've never been able to get Nick and Charlee a great Christmas like I had when I was growing up. I don't know how my parents did it but they did. I really wish not to speak to D anymore because it's over. Once my body has no desire for you, it's over. Again, I will not look for a mate. I don't even want to be sexually active anymore. It's too much of a fuckin hassle. But the desire will always be in me.

It's just I really want to know what real love feels like. To be in love. There is only one time I felt it. That was puppy love. So that's probably not even real. But it was a great feeling.

December 7, 2007:

I got straight busted today. I was trying to find something expensive that I could sell at a later date. When I was busted, all I could do was say hi and make up a story. It was quite funny, but my heart left for a minute. Everything else was put back in place, that I moved around. Anyway, it's so over. D blatantly is failing all subtle monetary tests that I'm giving him. I told him I may be riding the train this weekend because I have no gas in the car. He basically says nothing like a bitch. Doesn't even offer any solution. Fuck him!

December 9, 2007:

D and I had a very long, serious talk about this relationship. Finally he admitted it. We made a mistake by getting married. I was so relieved to hear him say it. Now I know for him it was also a control issue when he would get so angry when I wanted to come to West-end and be alone. He has been trying to convince himself that we were happy. Now I have to deal with, once again, being totally without Holiday money or cheer. I've been going through this for too damn long. I've got to get a 2nd job.

December 12, 2007:

It has been so beautiful in Atlanta since Sunday. Today will be the last very warm day, probably for the remainder of the year. I did not talk to D at all yesterday. I have no desire to at all anymore. Whatever physical, emotional, and mental desire that was there with him and me is gone completely. He's too weak and emotional, not to mention broke as hell. I really hope that one day his writing s and art work become known. His friend, A, is going to be staying with him for a couple of days. And his friend G will be coming to see him next week. I'm so glad. And I actually hope that he can reconcile with his true wife of 30 years. I actually think they will reunite what has been going through was a definite lack of physical pleasures from her. If he was physically able, I'm sure D would have tried to screw me every night. I wouldn't allow it because I know that at his age, it would have been too much for him. And I would have gotten repulsed with looking at his sagging body. I know its cold for me to even write that down, but I'd rather write then allow it to be said out loud to him. Anyway, as I've written, so often my favorite place in Atlanta on days like this is Piedmont Park. So peaceful was my walk yesterday. And I basically stayed outside all day. I hope I'm able to do that again today. My other favorite is the beautiful rest.

December 14th 2007

Well guess where the hell I am stuck on—the expressway. I guess D. will be getting the car back like he's been wanting to. It costs me too much for the gas anyway. Oh! What happened the car is basically just stopped. It's like something sucked the energy out of it. So I'm hoping the HERO will stop because I don't have my cell phone. I was late for work anyway. I hate this shit.

December 22nd 2007

I spent last night with D. of course we had the wine and cheese. We had physical contact, but for some reason I could not reach a climax. I slept well though. D. gave me some very much needed Christmas gifts. I didn't have any for him, but like any man me giving my body to him is his present. I'm home now, I'm so glad that I cleaned up real good Friday before I went to work. Charlee will be with her dad and brother for Christmas. El-Haaj and his family will be here Sunday at 5pm. I sure hope they bring some money with them because I have nothing to give or feed them. I was broke last year at this time and the year before that and the year before that. This fucked up pattern has got to stop. Anyway, I'm not sure about myself anymore. I always thought that I knew who I was. I thought I had re-invented myself after my failed suicide attempt two years ago. But I'm finding that I'm still lost. Like some type of unseen force has me by a rubber band. And just as my break-through (and I don't mean that in a spiritual sense) is right there literally touching the very edge of my finger nail. The force slings me back. And I again like fucking déjà vu find myself right here doing here doing exactly this and broke. With no real mean in my life that can emotionally comfort me or financially comfort me. No one can or shall I say no man will ever have my heart or trust again. Damn I really thought D. was the one. He's nothing, just white. I really trusted him and because I don't anymore I've been reading his diary. It's so amazing the more I write negatively about him, the more he writes about how he loves me. But he really doesn't love me just the physical. I also read that he was glad that the car broke down, that it's where it should be now—with him. And he told his ex-wife, she was pissed. I also read that he will always love her and he misses her, well after 30 years I sure hope he still loves me. He also writes about how he mistreated her. I always knew that because of the things he's tried with me. Well I'm hungry and a little tired, but mostly hungry. I have fucking nothing here to eat. God something has got to give. Why am I struggling with my life, ever since I was eighteen years old? I sure don't' wish this on any of my children. I really wish I knew who my real parents are. I believe it would help me know who I am, why I do the things I do, why I know I should be successful. My arrogance, my looks, my coldness, my stride—who the fuck am I? Why won't anymore tell me? I want to run so far away when I start to feel this way. I miss Charlee. I hope she as fun with her dad. She again tells me how much she misses Nick. I really hope his life is OK. I really hate their dad. I wish I could just make him feel the pain he's caused me, how abandoning feels, I really wish he could feel that. I hope one day I will be happy with myself. I really thought I was. I really don't know anymore at 42 years of age. God I'm hungry and I want to run. But Charlee keeps me here. I just want happiness, peace, comfort, and some mutha fucking money!!! It's sad but in two days' time money would help me with other things.

December 25th 2007

Well, I'm very calm I feel pretty much at peace. I really needed these days off from work. I've been sleeping a lot. El-Haaj and his family made it here by Greyhound on the 24th. He looks so handsome in his fatigues (Air Force) so tall and handsome. He's gained about 15 pounds. A is walking he and I spent a lot of time together. Oh I spent the first part of the 24th with D. he made sure that I got some presents for everyone. Anyway, back to the present N. seems to have lost weight. I really don't like her attitude. She's so damn Ghetto, I've never been to WATTS/ Compton California, that's where she is from. And she is beyond Ghetto. I really hate he met her. I wish he and G. could have made it work. Any way I know my son is not happy. I made sure to tell him not to have any more children by her. It would be a disaster for him. He shared with me that he has a domestic write-up on his Air Force record already. He said that him and N. got into an argument at her mother's house, N. called the police and the military police showed up. I found this out when we were walking from my job to see if he could rent himself a car. The young bitch (N. that is) started showing out at my job, cursing and saying "fuck you" to El-Haaj, apparently something happened and I missed it while we were walking through the building and she just exaggerated it. I was so embarrassed for El-Haaj, he looked like he wanted to cry. She walked across the street from us and that's when he and I really got a chance to talk and that's when I told him how she acted when she was here during the summer.

December 25, 2007:

Anyway, he's trying so hard to please her. I'm going to try and stay out of his business. I mean, he has to learn. But he definitely got married too soon. He's still innocent. When E and J arrived to pick them up to go to North Carolina, he was a little boy and she, E, turned into a little girl. They were wrestling with each other. My oldest daughter E is absolutely beautiful. She has the prettiest long black hair and her skin is flawless. J looks just like her. I'm so proud of her and Haajy too. I just hope he doesn't allow N to mess him up because I'm in no position to hole him in no way. I mean, I'm trying to figure out what's next for me. Anyway, E gave me a very nice hug when they left. J is beautiful. Very innocent. He's the perfect baby. I also see a lot of E in him.

Anyway, a lot of other things have been going through my mind. I need to pass the P.S.F. Exam and again look for another job with daytime hours so I can spend time with Charlee. I also need to get a second job. It's been a rough ride with dumb-ass D. He taught me that no matter what race a man is, a man will do anything to get a woman into bed. Wine . . . dine . . . and once they get you into the trap, you find out they're all the same men wanting sex for free. They don't really want to help with anything else. I've definitely outgrown D, so again I'm single and I like it. I've got to reinvent myself. I've been looking at myself in the mirror lately and I can't seem to find any attractiveness to me. I mean, I started wearing makeup two work. It's not looking attractive. I look, dare I say, old. Maybe I'm going through that 7 year change that the human body goes through. I can usually get my hair to look good, but that's not working either. I mean, I look worn out, even though I'm trying to go to the gym on a regular basis. Every time I get in a good rhythm at the gym, something fucked up happens. I knew D was full of shit about 3 weeks ago when I needed gas money and he kept saying he was broke. I'm so broke! "C needs money, I'm broke,, I tore up my credit card, It's gonna take me 5 years to pay my debt", he says. But while we were dating, he was pulling that damn credit card out like it was nothing. When I saw him yesterday, I was determined to get some money so he gave me $20.00. when I get paid, I will pay him for the phone bill ($25.00) and mail it to him. And after that, I really never want to see D again. Usually, when I'm done with a person, I delete their phone number from my phone. I've done that with D. so I tried to call him today, just to say Merry Christmas and I called the wrong number. I was glad. I want to view D as an interesting memory. The sooner I can make him a distant friend, the better. I'm going to rank him along with Nick and Charlene's Dad when I think of the men that have disappointed me the most. C is first and D is definitely second. It's because in my mind I thought he was different and I thought I was ready for companionship. I thought I was about to begin a life that I'd been trying to gain on my own. I know now what I have to do. It's going to be easy. I've been struggling too long. I'm going to have to make my own happiness. I now have no trust in men. I'm truly numb to them. There are no real men, or maybe it's me. I don't think so. I mean, what is it that I'm lacking all of a sudden?

December 30, 2007:

I've had a sort of interesting weekend. I mean, nothing spectacular has happened. I just feel myself literally waiting for something to happen for me. Something great in a good way to benefit me and my children. I made $32,000 dollars this year. I have no way to know what I've done with it. That's what's been so interesting about my weekend. I talked to my best friend C. and I told her I know what I need to do. I know I miss-manage my money something terrible. There's no damn reason why I shouldn't have more or at least something saved up.

I received a letter in the mail from D Saturday. He's basically begging for sex. I have absolutely no desire for D and another interesting thing, I actually talked to God very serious about D when I met him and I asked for guidance. I must have interpreted the guidance wrong because it was a disaster. He calls, I ignore his calls. I would really like to forget D. the more I continue to deal with him, the more meaningless he becomes to me. The disappoint I feel about him is so interesting. This disappointing feeling is actually a very strange sensation. I feel numb for men because they don't offer anything. I've expressed that already a couple of days ago. So what the hell is next for me. I'm feeling very lost again. I need a new type of stimulation in an intellectual making money type of way. There's got to be something out there for me. What on earth is holding me back? Well, I've taken something to help me relax. I feel like all I'm doing is rambling.

January 4, 2008:

Well, I finally had to really hurt D's feelings. I wrote him a four page letter in which I will put inside as an insert, but hopefully I will get closure from this disastrous relationship. My new year was good. I went to see the peach drop. I hate Nick and Charlee were not with me. I called D's ex-wife and left a message on her work phone to let her know this marriage was over and commended her for putting up with D's issues for 30 years. She was very nice. Her voice is very strong, so I was actually surprised that she allowed herself to be treated badly by D. Anyway, I'm ready to totally forget him. Someone will be out there for me, but I truly feel bitter towards men. Truly bitter. I really thought he was different and I'm starting to think that all men want is someone to take are of them.

I submitted a letter to my human resources department and I've asked to be transferred to another department. I'm not happy doing security anymore and I need to be with Charlee. Something has got to give. I'm getting frustrated again with life, but I'm holding on much better than 1.5 years ago, thank God. I'm pretty sure D is going to write me a letter. I'm going to send him another one this weekend.

January 14, 2008:

I'm a true failure at everything. That's the feeling I'm feeling at this very moment. Charlee still doesn't have any eyeglasses. I never went to renew her medicaid card. I didn't go to work today. I have 29 hours of sick leave. I'm so damn tempted to take it all. I think I'll take tomorrow off too. I just don't feel well mentally. There's got to be something in this world that can make me feel stable.

Acting class is going good this year. I decided to wear makeup and dress nice, but once again, my gym schedule is shot to fucking hell. I haven't been in a month. So I feel as though my body is not fit again. On a positive side, I had dinner ready for Charlee when she got home. The downside is that she didn't get home until 6:15.

I don't talk to God on a regular basis like I used to or should do. Sometimes I don't think he exists. I'm still struggling with everything. I get absolutely no respect at work. Everyday in briefing, I'm laughed at. Everything I bring up for training. When I said I wanted to get out of the security business, I should have done it. I don't feel fulfilled anymore in this business. And once again, I'm looking for another job. I really don't like people. I'll try something with Ranstat daytime hours. I haven't combed my hair since Friday and I don't give a shit either. I need a break through. I need something positive to happen in my life. I know I got up this morning. I'm breathing, walking, talking, but damn it! That's not enough anymore! And I'm feeling desperate now. Somethings got to give before I lose my mind again.

January 15, 2008:

I took another day off work. I'm glad I did. I went to the library. Sent in a job resume for administrative duties. Only something with high-tech security. Then I went to meet Charlee at school. And I embarrassed her by showing up, so I left. I got home at about 5:45. She was already here. I think she thought I was angry with her, but I know she's a pre-teen, so I didn't have an attitude. Later, she asked me if she hurt my feelings. I didn't say yes or no. I just told her that I knew she wanted to ride the bus with her friends, so that's why I left. We had dinner together again. It was nice. I miss her so much. She's growing up fast. It's only me and Charlee now. And I want to give her more quality time. God only knows how that's going to come about.

Anyway, when I put her to bed, she apologized to me again for hurting my feelings. That made me feel good, like she really does love me, because sometimes I wonder. Anyway, I started crying on the way home. I had to distance myself away from the other people at the MARTA station.

I know I have to go back to work but I don't want to. I'm really trying to get a grip on myself, but I struggle sometimes like you wouldn't believe. I'm still not feeling mentally strong yet. I was actually feeling dizzy today. Even while sitting down. I think I'm starting to have mild anxiety attacks again. I'm not happy with my job situation and it's starting to really bother me. Nick called me yesterday. I think he told me he loves me. All I can do is pray about his situation. I think that I may also be getting nervous about this monologue at my acting class. I want to succeed with this so bad. Why can't I fight like I used to? When I believe in this class and when I want, I don't want this to be a waste of my time, my money, or the instructor's time. I need for this to work for me.

January 25, 2008:

Well, I'm feeling strange as of this moment. Because I want my acting class to work out. But I can't seem to express emotion.

January 30, 2008:

I have so many thoughts running through my mind right now. Not really bad thoughts, just feeling indifferent about a lot of things. First, just let me thank God for my shift change. I took a step down and a pay-cut. That part I'm not happy about. But hey, I've got to rely on only me now. D solidified that for me. Proving that he's no better off than any other broke muthafucka. Just full of lies. I was supposed to do laundry this past Sunday but it was so beautiful outside. Just a tad bit windy, but gorgeous. And of course I was at my favorite spot, Piedmont Park. I walked home from there. My acting class went well. I actually got very positive comments from my instructor and the class reviewed ourselves on tape from two weeks ago. I looked great thank God. I put on makeup and decent clothes.

I went over to D's after work and I always read his daily journal. This man is really sick and continues to live in a fantasy world. Although I do admire that he does continue to write, sculpture, and plays his guitar, and writes songs, I really wished he would make an effort to sell his talents for the quick minute we were together. He only started making hand-made business cards and I think, but I'm not sure, he told me he was marketing his work at his job. Now I think that was all a lie. Something he was using to keep me. Or so he thought. This man is so pitiful and backwards.

I got paid Friday and became so fucking angry with him because I'm broke after paying bills and I know he has nothing to offer me. But a little hard dick and wine and cheese that has become so old to me now. When I think of D, I actually become nauseous. Now I don't want the bubble-headed impish skinny rat to touch me every again.

January 31, 2008:

After work today, I'm supposed to see W. I'm excited about that because I know all W can offer me is his body. But that's a good thing because I knew that 5 years ago. Although I do consider him a friend also. I'm at my regular post today. The garden and I love it. The funniest thing happened to me today. I always ask for water at Caribou Coffee and for a year, they've never charged me, but today they did. 50 cents! I saw N yesterday. We usually have a brief conversation. She tried her damnedest not to speak to me. I see all of the Engineer's in the morning. The only one that speaks to me now is Ghebru.

February 1, 2008:

Well, W came over yesterday. I'm going to have to let him go. I'm convinced even now more than ever that he's still with another woman. It took him 20 minutes to become erect and when he released, I didn't know it. And there was nothing to show that he did release. And he lost his erection real quick. So what I'm going to do is text him and break it off. I'm going to meet with the poor white impish trash today to get papers notarized.

March 23, 2008

Well, I'm officially divorced. I was actually hurt by the decree in the mail, but at the same time, I believed that I wasn't bound to D anymore. Even though D and I never moved in together (Thank God), I still felt bound to him, and it didn't feel good at all. I said a lot of hurtful things to D. You know, the really sad thing about what I said? I meant every word. I meant for him to feel every angry pitch and tone in my voice. I've often pondered why I was so angry towards him. The answer I keep coming to is after he gained my trust by giving me one hell of a summer courtship (a courtship I'll always cherish) he started to become psychologically abusive. I tried to handle it, but I couldn't help having flashbacks of when my first husband doing the exact same things to me. I was 18 years old and didn't know what was going on. I thought I was suppose to take it only to realize that after having 3 children back-to-back, never experiencing an orgasm, losing my hair, and at 5'8 weighing 95 pounds that I was being abused. And at the age of 42, I'll be damned if I am going to go through that again. My anger at D was quickly starting to turn into hate. There were times when I had to distance myself from him and even deleted his work phone number from my phone. The only thing that saved this relationship was the total care that he gives me when it comes to love-making in the raw sense. I mean, I've had some good lovers and I myself am an unselfish lover. This would explain a fatal attraction that I've had once upon a time. I digress. But D is beyond words. How can I let that go? A male friend of mine once told me never to let good dick go because men are not going to let good pussy go. A female co-worker of mine told me to start thinking about me, to receive my pleasures and not to feel guilty about it. Well, I don't! As long as D satisfies me, I'm his.

March 26, 2008

I haven't slept now in two weeks. I talked to D today. He's giving the Neon to Habitat for Humanity. He was never intending to get the car fixed. And something really simple is wrong with it. Anyway, I'm driving my $425.00 car A to Band sometimes C.

Anyway, all this week I've been at the garden desk and loving it. I hate changing. We go back to the rotating schedule next week. K has been really nice to me lately. I don't trust it because when I started on this shift he was actually treating me like the new kid on the block being really nasty to me. I wanted to quit. I took the CPO exam which I thought was stupid because if I was hired as a supervisor then I should be considered already qualified. It was a challenging test. In the 15 years I've been in security a lot has changed. There is a supervisors meeting Saturday but no one has told me to attend and I'm not going to ask. It's like they've basically taken me off back-up supervising positions for the weekends. I really believe G asked how much my check was the first and only time I was supervisor since leaving my second shift position, and did hourly and he took it away because of the amount my check was with the overtime. My check went from $1,243.00 to $1,123.00 after taxes. I now bring home $880.00 as opposed to the $989.00 which is one hell of a difference. But you know, I'm okay with that because it's out of my control. I'm home with my daughter, we eat together (not like we used to when we were a family, just me and her and N), but at least I'm home with my child.

A lot has really occurred in the last week. I had to get my number changed. I really hope Charlee does not give her daddy my number, that would really hurt my feelings. I just don't need to talk to him right now. He's a cruel, hateful IDIOT!!! And I really feel sorry for N. My sister, Aunt D. Ms. H, none of these people have my number because I know he will call and ask them for it. This past weekend, guess what happened to me? My home was broken i to and my car, (the one I left at D's), was also broken into. I left the window down and they took my canvas bag, my juice, and my cupcakes. At the house, they took one of the space heaters. But that person was caught from the crack house next door. In all of my adult life, that has never happened to me. And I hope never again. I am so grateful to be home with Charlee. Thank you to the Higher Power over all of us.

March 31, 2008

Well, I had a great weekend with D. I'm still very careful with my feelings for him. After all, I'm sure the contempt I felt for him when we were married, he had to also have some contempt for me too. It's only human. I'm actually kind of wired up.

April 2, 2008

The last time I wrote I was very wired up. So yesterday, the 1st of April, I came to D's, worked on my book, pondered over some things, and then I ran around the neighborhood. It felt great. I had to release some energy in another form.

There's a lot kind of going on at work, things I can't quite put my finger on. Well there is one thing. I didn't pass the CPO exam. I got 65% out of 100%. So, I got a feeling there's talk going on. Also, K asked me last week why I was arriving at work at 06:35/6:40. I couldn't even answer that I knew it was coming, so I reset my alarm for 05:00 hours instead of 05:40 hours, yep . . . a whole 40 minute difference. And now, I get to work between 06:28 and 06:30, which works for me. So fuck them! Anyway, I'm at D's and my book is coming along good so far.

I'm at home now. I am so sleepy. I'm in my room hoping I'll sleep good. I slept kinda okay last night/this morning. Just as I got into my room to sleep, my alarm came on. I had a pretty good day at work. I was at the dock entrance with horny toad Mr. G.

But what an absolutely beauty of a day it is, 76 degrees. Since I ran yesterday, I took today off. While I was at D's, I was tempted to go to the park, but something told me to come home. I'm so glad I did. Charlee arrived at 5:30 pm, just like she should.

I'm finding myself missing D. Wow! Who would have thought? The funny thing is he's started to go into his impish ways again. If I really am in love with him, I should be able to accept his strange ways. I so, however, admire the way his creative mind works. I've written that thought down before. The way he creates! We are so much alike in that way. I also envy the total peace his apartment has. The room he offers as my room is so calming. It's decorated Hindu style. A dark mysterious red comforter and pillow set decorates the bed, the walls have ancient Asian and Hindu artwork hanging on them. I really like that room. I don't think I've mentioned something that D is doing. He is heavily into church now, something he started doing when I believe he realized our marriage wasn't going to work. He would go to musical concerts there, but I think what really got his attention was Saint Marks, how architecturally stunning it is. And he always stared it when he walked me home from work . . . during our wonderful courtship. Anyway, when we were definitely going through it, he needed something to ease his mind (I think). And on the rare days that I was civil to him, he would tell me about his experience. He also began reading self help books.

There was the time when we went to file the divorce papers. I met him at the Georgia State train station. There he was, all impish looking with that fake "nothing is wrong" grin on his face. He immediately sensed that I was not happy. Shit! It was cold that day, I wanted to go home. I was tired, sleepy as hell, and still trying to get used to the day shift. He thought I was going to work afterward. Anyway, I had gotten paid that Friday and I was literally broke. My half of the processing fee was $44.00. I didn't have it and I was angry at myself because he was counting on me to have my half, but damn it, I was counting on him giving me and my two youngest children a comfortable life. This was something I yelled at him on the walk to the courthouse. His face turned red, but he held on to that fucked up "nothing was wrong" grin on his face. I wanted to push his ass in the street. I swear, the only thing that kept me from pushing him was the fact that he definitely would have gotten hit by a fast moving car and possibly killed. But what I saw was the hurt on his face, even with that shit eating fake as grin. He was feeling every word I said and I had to stop talking and collect myself from wanted to hurt this man. We finally get to the processing place, and I became angry again when I saw how meticulous he had put all of the paper work together. My first thought was "this lying, cheap ass, white mothafucka knew this marriage was not working but was hell bent on living miserably for God knows whatever reason". Then, I thought in my mind, "Thank God I was the Bitch I've been towards him because he probably knows I would have killed him". I never spoke those words to him though. Anyway, I think the name of the self help book he was reading was "Being Happy, No Matter What", and I do, with all of my heart, wish my sweet D nothing but happiness . . . with or without me. Preferably with me.

April 29, 2008

Well as always, when I wait for so long to catch you up on things, it's usually when I'm sleep deprived. And a lot has taken place. Not bad things, but dramatic things. So I'll start at this exact moment, so you can get the feel of where my mind and body are at this moment. I'm sleep deprived. I've been sleeping every other night very hard and sound and then I've been completely awake the next. So, as of this writing at approximately

6:50 pm, I'm at my home in the West-end in bed. I asked my beautiful preteen daughter if it was ok that I came to my room and she was ok with it. Anyway, as I digress with so much to tell you.

D and I have been heavily seeing each other again and for the past 7 weekends I have been at his home in midtown and loving every minute of it. My daughter Charlee, she's very perceptive. She figured out that that's where I've been going, so she spent the last two nights with D. Last night, which was Monday night, we had our usual wine and cheese with great conversation. We truly have a genuine friendship (I really like this man). Later I received a magnificent massage and that led to incredible love making. If I was a younger woman, I would probably be a fatal attraction to D. But I've never been that way to any of my other lovers, so I don't think I'll be that way with him. He is so attentive and such an unselfish lover. Damn!!! I mean, that in a good way. Anyway, he gave of himself so unselfishly last night that I found myself day dreaming of him throughout my work day. Damn!

Anyway, lets go back to Sunday night. Well, earlier Sunday I had to work 12 hours, so I had a lot to think about and I've finally realized that I'm in love with D. So I told him Sunday night after I put Charlee to bed in the room, where I usually sleep and the room that David refers to as my room. We had wine and cheese and I just told him that I was in love with him and I asked him not to ever hurt me. Damn! I fell asleep and my left hand has fallen asleep, so I'll finish the story tomorrow.

April 30, 2008

I cooked a great dinner for me and Charlee. It felt good to do that. Nick would have enjoyed it too. He always talks about my good cornbread. Anyway, back to the D and Menasha saga. Earlier this year, I started packing some of D's dishes that were still over here and I took them to his home. I wrote him a note and asked if he wanted his key back. He never responded to the question, so I never asked again. I just put it in my mind that at that time, I would just keep D for physical pleasures. The couple of times that I spent the night with him, he would be so child like and happy that I actually felt bad for him because at that time I only wanted physical pleasure and nothing else. But he would fix dinner for me, talk to me, massage me, calm me, make me feel loved, and be so damn outstanding. I also noticed that he had changed. He wasn't as whinny as before, or at all. He was actually more manly, in terms of his personality.

May 5, 2008:

I worked a half day today, but when I arrived to work I had a terrible attitude. It's been about 2 years since I've had the type of feeling I had today. I hated everybody because it seems as though everybody is after me again. I'm tired of this profession that I've chosen. It's such a fucking boys club and I just don't find satisfaction in it anymore.

May 6, 2008:

I think I might know one of the reasons I'm feeling fucked up. I've lost my storage unit and what little that was still in there. I hate it because of the bonds that were in there for safe keeping for my Uncle. And I think my original black and white shots. Damn it!

May 7, 2008:

I'm at work and it's 6:45 am. I haven't slept in about 5 days. Both my sons are fucking morons. I've heard that Nick is in Metro. I think that's like juvenile. H and that girl he married haven't been in Atlanta 2 days and they were both about to go to jail for fighting. They were about to take the baby to defacs. Both of them, H and N, need help. I think the damn light burned out in my car, the big headlights. I think all I need are bulbs. Well, I'll close for now. Until later.

June 8, 2008:

Oh! My God! Exactly a month has passed and you will not believe what has happened. I'll start with the fun good news. I took the kids to the company picnic at 6 flags and we had a blast. They are so beautiful (Charlee) and handsome (Nick) when they have on decent clothes. Anyway, my tolerance was great and I actually enjoyed the weekend with them, but I had my mind ready two weeks ago. I rode roller coasters and played games and bonded. I'm so going to miss them when they really grow and become adults. I pray for them to be successful. And that the world they build for themselves treats them well.

Anyway, D has started to become impish once more and again. I'm starting to hate that side of him. It turns me off! It usually starts when he becomes too clingy, then childish, then impish, then whiny. He really needs some type of counseling. He and I are scheduled to go on vacation for the 4th of July, so I've decided that I really don't want to spend any time with him until then. I mean, we will be together for 5 days in Charleston, S.C. When D gets that way, it's such a turn off. I can't even respond to him.

It's actually very selfish the way he gets. All of those ways I mentioned. Now that I really think about it. Because it becomes all about him. Those things. I've come to the conclusion that the paintings that he does as beautiful as they are, he's doing it to buy me; to keep me close to him. But, I don't understand why. I'm not the best looking woman, I'm not ugly either, but why has he focused on me like he has? Soon I hope this will come to light because rarely do I verbally tell him I love him. I go through phases where I can't stand him. I know that waking up to him every morning or looking at him while he sleeps is not something I can do for the rest of my life. He sleeps naked and curls up like a baby. He's pale and clammy in the morning, not an attractive picture. And sometimes he looks like an old ass woman. So what the hell is this relationship for then? Well, it's something that I need to search inside of myself for. I'm settling because I'm lonely sometimes. If this was purely for sex then I would be at his home now. I mean, even when C was mean to me I still loved looking at him as he slept. When I knew W was fucking another woman, I still loved looking at him as he slept. When I knew W was going home to his wife, I loved looking at him as he slept and all of these men had ways that hurt and pissed me off. But it never took away my desire for them. So is it me with the problem or is it D? The search must go on.

June 9, 2008:

It's so nice to be home. I talked to D today but I forced myself to do so. I wish I knew what this relationship means to me.

June 11, 2008

Ok, it's official! I'm feeling truly uneasy about something. I hope it's not the job. I thought maybe it was my menses trying to start but I don't think that's it. Also, I don't seem to miss being with D. That doesn't bother me a lot! I'm that untrusting of other people that I'm forcing myself to try and love this man. Something that should be a genuine feeling in a relationship. I can't seem to find my brother. We usually talk much more frequently. The times that I've called! His phone is free after 7 pm Las Vegas time, and the last couple of times I've tried to call, including yesterday, his phone has not been on. And of course, the same feeling of hurt and abandonment of finding out 10 years ago that my parents weren't really my parents and that all of my childhood, especially the unhappy times, could have possibly been avoided, rise again.

If only my mother (adoptive) would have kept her promise to my birth mother and allowed her to visit me every now and then (that's what my aunt D told me). The memory that that was supposed to be with the arrangement, the memory of that lady walking past Mama C's house when I was very very young and waving at me will always haunt me. It had to be her, at least she did try. I remember looking for her several times after that, but I never saw her again. But I'm going to put into words her description. She was tall, slim build but with hips, long hair, about my complexion, and pretty. I think that she would put me in the mind of my oldest daughter E. Sometimes I wonder if she is still alive and if she is still capable of looking for me. Does she ever wonder about me still? If she is still alive, I would guesstimate her age at 60-62 years old. That gives me hope. But the more years pass by, the older we both become and the inevitable happens. I so miss my father. I wish he was still here. I miss my house on Beecher Street. I drive by now without feeling so betrayed by R. I even wave or blow the horn at her. Well, maybe these words that I've written down will ease my mind a little. It always help when I write.

June 16, 2008:

Work was okay today. Even though I did not sleep last night. 5 am Came so damn quick. When I got home today, I took a nice nap. My neighbor asked to use my phone 10 minutes. It ended up being an 1.5 hours. Needless to say I had to look for her because anytime I use my phone, you have to go up the street. I was not happy with her. That will be the last time she uses it. When a person tell me 10 minutes, I take them at their word.

I also went to D's after work. He's been busy painting. Finally, I'm starting to miss him, but in the physical sense. I'm still very unsure about this relationship. At this time, it's 90% me not sure what it really means to be in a relationship, what is really suppose to go on. I need clarity on this thing. Is it about looks? I mean, aren't I at my age supposed to be over that? Aren't I? When I think about D, I'm starting to see how much older he looks and wimpish he looks, and impish. I'm not the best cut cookie in the bunch. I have so many cosmetic flaws that I'm surprised D dates me. Fuck! I just don't fucking no about this shit! I hate it when I get cluttered with thoughts like these.

It was my intentions to visit D yesterday for Father's Day. However, my menses started Saturday thank goodness because I don't want to be like last year on the 4th of July. Anyway, it has been very heavy and I just couldn't move yesterday. Not because I was in pain, but because I was truly drained. I literally laid around all day. I did a couple of cosmetic things around the house, listened to my gospel music, framed some items with frames that D bought me, looked at pictures of my Dad. I do miss him and my mother. I mean, they did the best they could. We had it a hell of a lot better than other children. Our own room, food everyday. It's just my mom could be something between "Mommy Dearest" and a very haunting movie that came on, "Flowers in the attic". That was so much like our mother in a lot of ways. We just weren't subjected to poisonings.

There is so much potential in me and I want to write a book so bad. I've always liked to write. I've always kept a diary. Ever since I could write. I've never been afraid of putting my deepest emotions on paper. Unfortunately, it's another story when trying to act them out. But I've gotten so much better. I was so proud of myself. This past Saturday in acting class this emotional piece that I've been working on, I memorized it! I showed promising emotions and I did excellent. And to me, that's all that matters. I see so much improvement in myself. Since my little mishap 2.5 years ago, I really feel closer to God. I know there's a higher source now. I'm still very conscious though of all my arrogant nature because it gets in my way sometimes. I've noticed that when I feel it coming on I can control it better. I need to so I can keep a job. So I won't be the cause of me blocking my own blessings.

It actually feels nice to be at this place. I do feel a sense of peace. And yes, it is scary because it really means that I'm getting older. I'm aging and I just want to do it gracefully and successfully and with faith and happiness. Well, I've written down what I was feeling. Hopefully I will rest better tonight.

June 17, 2008:

I had an easy day at work because I was very sleepy around 10 am Read a very beautiful letter from D and it made me sad that sometimes I don't seem to view this relationship the same as he does. And that I write such harsh things about him. I'll try to see things different.

July 7, 2008:

Well, there's a lot, I mean an immense plethora of a tale that I must tell. But not at this moment. I am however going to say that I've gone to one of America's most haunting places. I mean that in the most beautiful way. I am also going to say that at some moments on my vacation I felt it hard to be with D. I mean that in a not so pleasant way. It may be a couple of days before I give the full account but I must arrange everything that I experienced in my mind so I can share it in the most telling way.

July 19, 2008:

Okay, I'm back. Much longer than a couple of days, huh? Well, I think it was for the best. I've had some time to think about D in a more positive light. Anyway, I am once again without personal transportation. It is my fault really. I was flying like a bat out of hell going to work last week and hit a bump in the road. Well I tore the transmission up. It was sluggish anyway (the transmission) which is why I never got a tag or tune-up. But I didn't become as upset as I should have or as I usually do. I just walked to work from Murphy Avenue.

I finally told D about the car Friday when I went over to his house. He seemed to have been more upset than I was.

Wednesday, we finally had a talk about getting me some transportation. He will probably end up getting me a Vespa. Those run about 1500 to 1700 dollars.

Anyway, after the ride home from the vacation, I wanted to come home. So from Sunday at 11:30 pm To Friday, I was at my home and I had a chance to really ponder on some things about myself and D. I have come to a conclusion. D, in his own twisted and strange way, really is in love with me. However, I do believe that 70% is lust on his part. I also believe that he has realized his mistakes from last year. That he really enjoys making me happy. But he's still trying to make me like him and that makes me dislike him. I was starting to feel bad about some thoughts I was having.

July 20, 2008:

Now about the trip. First of all, I wasn't that impressed with the room D claimed he paid $100.00 a night for. If he did, he was definitely cheated. He kept referring to it as a motel. That further confirms my beliefs that D is not as sophisticated as he thinks he is. The room was $69.00 a night. It was what one would expect, but for a hundred I was about ready to complain at the time I walked in the door because the first thing I smelled was smoke. And I saw a lot of cosmetic flaws. Anyway, we changed clothes, took a ride downtown which was about three miles away. That was perfect though. I loved taking the ride in. We ate at a restaurant named Nick's. The food was great! I had a vegetarian plate of cabbage, greens, potato salad, and baked beans with tea and water. He had a salad because the food was cooked with great authentic ethnic seasoning (pork and fatback). Then we took a walk through downtown to Battery Park. We ended the town walk with a beautiful walk through some of the oldest mansions in the U.S. Older than the White House. These houses were so high they made some of Atlanta's oldest mansions look quite small and not as elegant. But I love my city. Anyway, we walked these very quiet and lovely old neighborhoods and we were both surprised that no one was enjoying their beautiful 3 story screened in porches that ran the length of the houses on each level. My mind immediately went to a place of physical pleasures I would be having on the top level of the porch. I wish sometimes that if only for a day or two that I could step back in time, invisible of course, and just see how the people lived. How they enjoyed these opulent mansions and gardens. Just to see the original signers of the Declaration of Independence and their hair styles, clothing, speech patterns. The women I'm most intrigued with. These powerful white men must have had other women. The wives probably knew of it. Maybe like the women of today. They had some mind set of don't bring a disease home and as long as the bills are paid, everything should be okay. There must have been happy families and very unhappy families living from paycheck to paycheck. I can only imagine. It was probably pure hell for the slaves which is why I would have to be invisible. I am a woman of color.

On another day we went to the Boone plantation. This is a place that all young children of color should see. God knows if I become very wealthy, I would sponsor a trip for inner city children to visit this place called slave row. It was depressing, yet uplifting because Master Boone did allow these slaves a bit and I mean just a bit of self preservation. They had a church. The slaves with special skills all had a house about the size of my porch to live in, but about 16people to a house. That was depressing to see. The original pictures of these slaves were heart breaking. The men and women were never as old as they looked. One of the small houses ha an original bed and set-up. Archeologist found small beads from necklaces that some of the women made trying to hold on to their African roots. It was quite heart breaking. But at the same time, people of color have come one hell of a long way. But we are so fucking lost at the same time. I wonder about certain acquaintances that I have who are very wealthy. Their children attend prestigious schools. These are the black children that have no idea and probably would laugh at something like Boone plantation because of their ignorance. If I learned anything from slave row, it's that Nick and Charlee need to see it. And it only makes me want to find out even more about my true ethnic background.

I took in a live performance about plantation life from a beautiful Gullan woman who lives in the Carolina low-country. A place that I would love to live for about a year just to learn the language. I bought a book about the language and would love to speak it. Sandra, the actress that gave the performance, was beyond words. You would have to see this performance. I can't put it into words, this performance. I will say that the visit to Boone is very expensive, but worth it. I hope and pray that I will be able to get Nick and Charlee there. I also saw a 600 year old tree and I took lots of pictures of one of the most hauntingly beautiful drive ways in the world. 97 live oaks that lap over each other. It took 200 years for that to occur on each side of the driveway. Absolutely breathtaking! Inside, the mansion was beautiful. That's why I want to just step back in time, just to see the entertainment of these people.

One of my favorite destinations was the great Atlantic Ocean. To see her in person, on land, was the scariest moment in my life. But the water was so warm. I finally got up enough courage to step in it. I collected so many seashells. The only way I can describe that experience is God himself. The power is indescribable. And I feel very blessed to have placed my feet in such awesome power.

The fireworks were great. We saw them all over Battery Park. Patriots point had them come off the ship. People in their private yachts were allowed to get as close as possible and I might add the great Atlantic at night is beyond black. The slaves coming over must have prayed to die. I can definitely understand why some jumped ship and killed their babies.

Fort Sumter is definitely scared ground to me now. And even more so because my father and brother are military men. This is another one of those places words cannot do it justice. You have to see it. But it brought me to tears because I've studied about this place. In Elementary school and High school and the History Channel always has specials on it. Oh yeah, it sits right in the Atlantic. Very haunting! I really felt the spirits of the men.

To sum up the whole trip, it was great. I hope one day soon I can take my two youngest children. They need to experience history.

I don't want them to be so lost to the world that they forget where some of these ancestors landed and from there made it to Mississippi. So if anything, I'll dedicate this trip to Nick and Charlee until I can physically get them there.

August 22, 2008:

Well, I seem to be on a pattern of writing once a month. And as always, there's a lot to tell, and as always I will try not to babble too much. I will start from the most recent incident that took place about two hours ago. Yes, at the job! As you already know, I was let go from a job 3 years ago because of the ignorance of another black person. Well at this job I refuse to let it happen to me again. But apparently, my self assuring ways again seem to intimidate the black man. Because once again I've bumped into the ignorant black male. I became so enraged today at him that I had to talk to my boss, the director. He, the director, assured me that I was not being reprimanded or punished for coming to him, that he had been made aware of the issue when it first occurred about a month ago. But like me, he was hoping that it would dissipate on its own. Well it didn't. And I knew it wasn't and I went to the director. And I'm hoping it will now be resolved. Dare I say by the white man because two persons of color couldn't do it. That is so damn embarrassing to me. Anyway, enough of that.

Charlee is really starting to rebel against me. She really is so much like her father.

August 24, 2008:

Okay, I'm back. It's been hard for me to concentrate. I didn't tell you that I had to leave work early Friday because of a co-worker that is making me have flashbacks, if you will, of the work environment at CNN. I refuse to be bullied by another black male. I cannot have two enemies. Both white and black. I'm becoming more and more confused as to my loyalties when it comes to a work and personal environment. Let me explain myself. I do not love D. I can't! He's too child-like and again impish. He's not consistent in his male adult behavior. He will be like a grown-up for a minute and slip into that 5 year old child-like behavior. It's sickening, literally. I can't bare for him to touch me anymore or kiss me. I think I'm bored with him. He's always trying to satisfy me materially, like a fucking child. I mean the gifts he gives are focused on my craft and he bought the scooter. But I can't repay him with love. I don't feel it. And yes it is hurtful that I feel this way. Love has to be mutual. Apparently I've yet to meet that truly special someone.

I must share something. Wednesday of last week one of my most coolest, dearest, most charming, love of my life took me to pick up my new uniforms. We talked about the relationship that we had. This is the only man since my father that I freely say I love you to. No one else, not even E, did I say those words to and mean it. Anyway, he looks great healthy. He still has it, that cool swagger that always made him look so manly. That take charge tone of voice without the dictatorship that so many black men I've talked to seem to think they need. W, W always have my love and always will have control of me because he knows how to be in control without the need to force it. That's what a woman like me needs. Also, earlier in the week I browsed through my grandmother's Bible, not to read the holy word but to look at all the letters and cards from 20 years ago, even 35 years ago. I found a letter that I wrote to God about the two H's and how I didn't like the younger H. Basically at age 17 I knew a weak man even then. Later on, more of the present 2006, I wrote a letter expressing my being bored with sex.

August 24, 2008:

Wow! And here I am again full circle. Bored with sex and weak men. What's a girl to do?

Re-group to get back into the gym, get my body right, and my head on straight. Figure out what to do about D.

August 28, 2008:

Well I didn't get a part in Fiddler on the Roof. But I wasn't expecting to get on either. The audition was so much fun though.

D is such a fucking drama queen. D sent me this formal letter in the mail telling me I didn't get a part. Sometimes he just over-does it. He called me about 15 minutes ago. I don't know what the hell he could have wanted at 10 o'clock at night. So I didn't say anything. I have two men on my mind to talk to him right now.

August 30, 2008:

I have every thought in the world going through my mind tonight. I feel very creative but I'm not sure what I'm supposed to be creating. As

I've written so many times, please forgive me for I'm about to babble. It's the hottest, most humid month in Georgia and I am now positive that lightening bugs have been extinct in my home town for about 13 years. Where did that thought come from? Well, tonight I was walking home from the west-end train station and the void of those beautiful flashes of light from millions of God's little creatures was just profoundly absent. I've always, always, always loved lightening bugs from the first time I can remember seeing than and that's when I was about 4 years old at my Grandmother's house. Also, remember starting up in the front of the yard of the house I grew up in that beautiful oak tree and every tree on Beecher Street towards the golf course. It seemed like stars came down from heaven and flashed just for me. As I sit and write, I wonder if there is anyone else that misses them. Do they feel the void? Is it as profound for them as it is for me?

And then there's D. Why is it when women want something in a man and they find half of it, but then the other half of the man kills the half that you were looking for? Why, why, why does this happen? There must be a happy medium. Once again, what the hell am I going to do about D?

Have I always fucked up at my job? Why am I always fighting the black male? Do I really intimidate them that much? Is it a flaw that I cannot seem to shake? What am I going to do for my career if I can't be a submissive woman in a mans profession? I must find what it is I'm supposed to create?

My left wisdom tooth has been determined to have a cavity. Yes, it needs to be extracted. I'm scared out of my wits to have another tooth taken out. Oh, don't get me wrong! The relief after the tooth is extracted is heaven sent but the preparations to have the bastards taken out is a form of torcher in my opinion.

September 17, 2008:

I'm convinced that I would have been one hell of a man. But for some odd reason God decided that I should be a female with a knack for arrogance and low tolerance for bullshit. I have a presence with men that seems to want them to tame me. I have a presence with women and they seem to be unreasonably jealous of me. Damn if only I had the money and power to go with all of this unreasonable power that people have given to me. Most of the time I find it quite amusing and sad for the people that give me so much power. Other times, it angers me.

November 27, 2008:

I'm at D's, I'm not sure if I hate being here because I'm lonely, or because I feel like I have nowhere else to go outside of Nick and Charlene's I feel I have no genuine love. D is pathetically in love with me and it sickens me to the point of unattractiveness towards him. I sometimes feel as though he's just lonely all the damn time. Shit! I hate Holiday's! And that he likes me around as a pet, and Charlee as a toy. Right now it's just he and I in his apartment. Any other time we would be completely naked and he would be doing whatever necessary it takes to please me. But I have no desire for that at this moment and the sad thing is, is that he would drop everything he's doing if I asked him to come and touch me (he's painting right now). That's not what I need. Fuck! I don't know what I need. Maybe it's the damn Holiday. I want to go home and look at my television. Be in my own environment. I so wish I could have all of my children with me at the same time. It's only happened once. Thirteen years ago in the summertime. Since then my 3 oldest children have gone through dramatic changes and my two youngest children are for the most part still innocent of loneliness. I wish I could talk to my brother. It's been about 8 months (maybe not quite that long) but I believe that he's fine. Perhaps he's found someone and enjoying life. He should! He deserves it.

November 30th, 2008:

Guess what I'm doing? I'm in bed at D's in the room he refers to as my room and Charlene's room, but I'm wide awake. I slept exceptionally well last night so therefore I'm well rested and going through my normal insomniac phase of being awake for a week and then sleeping for 12 hours when my body begins to shut down. Anyway, that's why I'm wide awake and very happy and fulfilled that I had a lengthy conversation with my oldest daughter. She sent me a picture of J. He's beautiful! And my oldest son, ElHaaj and I spoke with A. He's beautiful too. And I spent hours talking with my best friend and eating at Ihop and then spending a very fun time with Y at her mothers house. It was great to finish the Holiday weekend this way. Anyway, needless to say, yes I had a Thanksgiving Holiday with D. I fought it with all my being but I felt sorry for him and no I didn't want to be alone this year. I wanted to be with my children and their children so bad. I ached for them. So I took a long hot shower Thanksgiving morning and tried to figure out how to get away from D. But I needed something so selfish. I asked for a hot oil massage from him in a very sultry voice. I told him I needed something to make me feel better. That really was the truth. So he made haste and put away all of his painting supplies, washed his hands like a surgeon. Something he must do before he touches me. He gave me the massage from heaven. He didn't say a word, he just massaged me from head to toe. It was perfect and lasted forever and forever and forever. Well, needless to say I was of a sound mind after three hours of intense physical pleasure, however, I noticed that he had a very sad look on his face. And he had every right to look that way. There have been so many times for the lack of having a better way of saying this that I've literally loved him and left him and he wouldn't hear from me until two days later. I knew that's what he was thinking. Just seeing his face look that way, I felt really sorry for him. So I made him feel at ease and we laid together and talked very quietly to each other. Yeah, it's kind of nice to get in touch with the woman in me because D can be such a bitch sometimes. The day was very sunny and spring-like so we had a glass of sherry and wine and cheese on the front porch and afterward took a very romantic walk in Piedmont Park. And to myself, I thanked God that I spent the day with him.

While we walked we had sweet potatoes on the stove so I could make us a couple sweet potato pies when we arrived home. We were both in the kitchen preparing our Thanksgiving meal. I had baked chicken, beets, sweet peas, garlic rice, a whole-wheat roll, a special red wine that he bought just for this dinner. And yes, my pies were perfect!

We had a candle lit Thanksgiving dinner. It could not have been more perfect and meaningful. I really felt loved by D and I felt like I could really give him my heart. Well, I will end for now. I still must tell about a beautiful vacation D and I had in October 31, 2008.

January 17, 2009:

Hello! It's been a while. I feel that now I only write when my thoughts can make since and after I've comprehended events that have taken place between long periods of time.

I'm at my home in the West-end, me and Charlee. And it's taken damn near 48 hours for my home to heat up. From what the weather people say, it's been this cold in Atlanta for two nights in a row. It's been 12 degrees with a wind chill of 0. but it's good to be in my own environment for a couple of days.

I have a 3 day weekend. Monday is Martin-Luther King Day. Tuesday is the biggest event in the history of the world, 2nd to the birth of Christ. The first man of African ancestry has become the U.S. President. This event is so nerve-wracking to me that I've chosen not to watch this event on T.V. and not to listen to any of the radio broadcast. I'll read the papers the next day if I find one. I'm very proud of this moment and I'll pray for our new president and his family. They have to be as scared as I am right now.

Well, on to other events. On December 12th, 2008 at approximately 3:57 pm I was hit by a car while riding my 50 cc scooter. I suffered a broken left collar bone. D was the first person I called. He was truly my knight in shinning armor. And as of this writing I am still recuperating from the injury. Though, I am not in as much pain and am able to bathe myself and move my left arm. I only cried once. That was in the emergency room when the pain became unbearable. It was the night of the Christmas party (Portman Holdings). D and I were in the E.R. For 5 hrs. we left out at 9:30 pm, got to the party at 10:30 pm I was determined to see the terracotta soldiers. It was well worth it. I hope to see them again before they go back to their home in April. Word traveled fast throughout Suntrust about my accident and people have been very kind in wishing me a speedy recovery.

My Christmas was beautiful. I spent it with D this year. It was almost a no go. I longed to be alone, but I twas good to be with D and his son on Christmas day. But at the same time, I really missed my parents and I longed for the yearly celebration we had every year at my Uncle's house called Christmas Tree. And I wished for my two little boys. How I long to have them know me and hug me and I can hug them and have them for the summer or weekends like I sued to have with my grandmother, Momma C. It hurts when I think that I'll never be able to know them so I love them from a distance and look at their pictures.

Nick and Charlee finally made it over to D's for Christmas. D bought them both MP3 players. They pretty much got what they wanted and I was pleased with their reactions. I am, however, not pleased with my youngest son. He's a petty thief now. He stole D's condoms and then he stole money from Charlee. So I've pretty much decided I really don't want Nick to spend the weekend at either residence for a while.

May 20, 2009

Good news. I purchased a lap top computer (Dell). I'm very proud of myself. My friend, W, and I talked for a while. I haven't seen D in about 2 weeks and I'm okay with it. I'm not sure at all about our relationship. This alone time is going to help things through. And I'm unemployed again, but it's okay because I did nothing wrong.

And my youngest Son, Nick, has truly gone from bad to worse. My sister referred to me as everything but the child of God. Nick is with her. He's gotten his Dad put out of their complex. I refused to have Nick at my place because I don't have custody of him.

June 27, 2009:

The lightening bugs are returning. It's been the most beautiful sight I've seen in a while. I've been seeing them at Piedmont Park.

Well, I am at a stale mate with the book and I'm trying to write. I think it's because I'm trying to write it as a book instead of doing what I'm doing right now, write from the heart.

I have finally come to the conclusion that I must work for myself. I am at at total loss for the desire to look for work in my field or any other field. I need freedom from bosses and boyfriends or whatever kind of relationship D and I have. I had a strong feeling tonight that we may not work out, again. But I could be wrong.

Charlee hurt me so bad. All I could do was cry. She got suspended from summer school. She's been acting out from my understanding since she started on June 15th. She says it's because she doesn't like the way the teachers are talking to her and the other student. I understand what she feels. And I had to tell her it gets worse. Your bosses are going to talk to you that way. Any kind of way people are not going to like you and the world is a cruel ass place and she's going to have to get used to it. I'm not going to keep taking up for her. It's time for her to grow up.

It hurt me to say those things in the way I said them, but pretty soon, 5 years will be here and gone and I'll be 50 years old. In the blink of an eye! And I just want my two youngest to be okay because I can't stomach Atlanta too much longer. I'm still trying to figure out if I want D with me at 50 years of age.

I've started back running on a pretty good schedule. I can tell D doesn't like it, but I've had to tell him this is my body and I wasn't liking my mid-section. And of course he said any man would say that weight looks good to him. D does something that gives me the creeps. He always grabs me or hugs me around my stomach. I hate that! I don't like the way it feels when he does that. It's almost like he's checking to see if I'm getting fat. Now when was really out of shape 6 months ago, we would be in intimate moments. He would actually grab the extra weight on my stomach and I was very turned off by it. I was totally turned off and couldn't wait for it to be over with. Now that I'm getting my 6-pack back he can't grab my stomach because it's getting flat again. Then he also tries to tire me out every night. I just laugh to myself and still get up and go run and it feels fantastic. D is still trying to be in control of everything with me. I'm trying so hard to understand this behavior. I'm going to have to have a talk with him again. He had gotten a lot better at letting me be, but he started reverting back when I lost my job. I actually think he likes the fact that I'm not working. Not because he's taking care of me. Believe me, he can't. I believe it's because he feels superior now. He thinks I'm going to ask him for money. He's offered but nothing has come of it. And I'm not going to bring it up. He offered on his own. I was looking very tired earlier this week. My hair was a mess and that's when he asked if I needed or wanted anything. I said no. I just need to get my hair done as a thought, but I will later this week. I'm just lazy. He quasi-offered saying he was going to sell a set of his paintings and give me the money for my hair. That was Tuesday. I've always felt that if a person really wanted to do something for someone and that person asked and/or offered, the offering that was needed then it should have been offered sometime during that day by the person who offered. That's why I never offer anything that I don't mean. And that's why I came home, because I knew D was about to get in that ignorant arrogant mood of his. I'm so glad I have my own place.

June 29, 2009

I'm having a real hard time this morning. I've slept great the last two nights on the sofa in the living room but this morning was bad. I guess I'm having a reaction from receiving my last paycheck in the mail and papers releasing me from my medical insurance.

It just feels like I can't get this job thing right. I keep playing over and over again what went wrong on my part. What game did I not play right? Who's ass did I not kiss? Who's ass was I supposed to kiss? Is this destined to work every two years? What's wrong with me? Why do people either love me, hate me, want to control me, half-way like me, think I'm weird, think I'm weak, think I'm slow, and most of all take me for granted? I took M's number out of my phone. I don't think he ever really liked me. I believe he was the main reason I was written up (I'm so glad I didn't sign that paper). He is definitely 2-faced but R told me that when I started on the first shift. I'm really hurt about losing this job. When I was fired from CNN I was very angry, but I didn't lose my work confidence. But with the loss of this job, my confidence is gone. I really do feel like a failure! I hope this feeling passes. I know that I'm feeling this way because I'm such a schedule-oriented person, even though most mornings I struggled getting up due to my chronic insomnia. I had a purpose!

I really, really wish there was a way to make people who have all decision making power over other people feel the pain. The mental pain, the monetary pain, and everything that goes along with being powerless under someone else. It feels like it brings you to a point of death. And just when they see that void, the sinking black hole brings them back. I bet that would change a lot of senior managers and on up. But I know that these people revel in that power. They sleep so good at night because they are untouchable. They really are. I sometimes try to make myself feel beret and say everybody falls from grace, that God doesn't like ugly. They'll get theirs! They never do! So many people that have done me wrong still have it going on. Their jobs, money, cars, house, good times, friends, and their sanity. I try so hard to not hate these people, but I do. I despise them! I've tried to kill them with kindness as my mother used to say, but that is wearing thin.

I'm starting to get sleepy, but I need to run. I need to keep my body in shape. D, I don't know what to do about him. I was supposed to go over yesterday for wine and cheese in the park, but I ended up seriously hibernating in the house in front of the TV. I actually enjoyed the alone time. I reflected a little bit and realized that I will be 44 years old in a couple of months and how time is whizzing by at the blink of an eye. Where will I be when I'm 50 years old? Where? Who will I be? Will I have a damn job? I can't depend on D. he's just too damn weak! He's caught up in nothing but sex with me. That's one of the reasons I didn't see him

Sunday. I really didn't want him to touch me. I'm starting to cringe when he does. It's because of how he acts. That child-like behavior is sickening. The man needs therapy. I mean damn! He's almost 60 years old. 85% of D is more of an impish child than he is a man. I can't take it too much longer. If he had more to offer than eating my pussy good, then maybe I can deal with it. But this is getting old again and real fast. Well, I'm going to end this and clean my house and try to get a run in.

June 30, 2009:

Well, I ran this morning. It felt great. I didn't run yesterday, but I did clean my house very well. Then I went to the store to get my watermelon and went to sleep all day. I got up at 9:30 pm And walked the belt-line and then I walked over to my father's house on Beecher and sat on the wall and reflected a little. I saw quite a few lightening bugs in the old neighborhood. When I saw on the wall, somebody must have been in the dining room because I heard a female voice call somebody named Corey to someone who sleeps in the front room. Then I got up and walked up Beecher and back to S. Gordon. I ended up going to bed at 2:30 am

I got up at 8:30 am This day and by 9:30 am I ran. I got home at 10:30, ate my melon at 11:15 and laid back down. I contemplated going over to D's but I'm actually enjoying my home. I know he is beyond pissed off at me but I just don't feel like being bothered with him all day. He's off work until July 6th. We usually go on a trip but it will be later on.

July 8, 2009:

Something happened to me that threw me off. SH called and asked me what was going on because I hadn't used the resume service he supposedly paid $20,000 for. I told him that I was still trying to heal from not having my job. He asked how they could be of help to me. So I asked him what I should say when asked why I left my last job. He tried the same bullshit head game. His reply was "what is it that I want them to say"? I told him that's why I'm asking him and he said if I find something and the question comes up, just let him know what I say so he can be on the same page. And I basically told him what I've been saying since this bullshit with them (the security depot) started. I probably won't work in this field again. So, unfortunately, my hurt was taken out on D. I really hurt his feelings. I had become tired of him anyway a couple of days earlier, but I was trying to get through it. So the call from S and my menses was very mean. To top things off, he saw me and Charlee with all our things basically running out of his apartment. And I swear, he looked like he was going to cry. I really felt bad. Sometimes I really miss D. usually my first day back at my house I do. This relationship is still confusing for me because my feelings for him fluctuate almost daily. He tries so hard and sometimes too hard to be perfect. And he has separation anxiety when I come to my home. It's like he's devastated. And then I start to feel really bad for him, almost sorry for him. That's not what this relationship is supposed to be about. Aren't I supposed to want to be with him just as bad?

It's not quite that way yet and I keep waiting for that. I also keep waiting for that strong feeling of love. That undying love that I've only experienced once. I only at this moment have undying love for my children and my two little DNA strands. So that's where the continuing confusion comes in. I work on it.

July 12, 2009:

Wow, this is beautiful. It started out as dry lightening, the most dangerous kind. I'm sure I've heard that said by Glen Burns. Anyway, I'm sitting here on D's porch. Well, the door way to stay away from the lightening. This beautiful summer storm is finally coming through. It's a warm/cold funny feeling wine. A tornado, I'm sure, has touched down somewhere. The rain started out very warm. You know those big drops? But still there was some sun out. This started at about 6 pm And it was 90 degrees. Hot as hell, humid. I absolutely love it. If I could be naked and sweating, I would.

Anyway, this beautiful hard summer rain just starting coming down, the wind has turned more gentle, the thundering and lightening still sounds very strong. I see the lightening, the sound of the rain. Oh it reminds me of when I was a child at the house I grew up in and the lights would always go out. My grandmother or my mother would always tell us to be quiet and listen to God's work. We would laugh but it's true. This is God's work.

I hope God isn't too angry at me though. I'm sitting on D's porch, drinking fine Italian wine; half-full in a 16 oz wine goblet. Oh the rain, thunder, and lightening still strong. It's absolutely beautiful. Now I can't help but wonder if my cousin was at 6 flags. If so, she and the people that may be at Piedmont Park are soaked to their drawers. But once you get wet in this rain, it actually feels good. Like your soul has been cleansed with God's water. I'm so loving this. It's absolutely beautiful.

July 16, 2009:

Well I bought another car. This one seems to be in better shape than the old one I had earlier this year. In one day I unloaded $1,300.00. I went ahead and got the tag and insurance the same day. Oh, I bought the car Monday of this week. D was astonished and a bit unhappy because me and Charlee can really come and go as I please without the hassles o MARTA. I still have the bike. It's locked in D's storage. I do miss riding it. It's a different sort of freedom on the bike. To me it's like I'm riding a mechanical horse. The attitude that comes with it, the helmet, nobody can see your face but they know you're a female. I always get a lot of comments from guys. They tell me how sexy I look when I straddle the bike while getting on and off. I think it's funny when they say that because that's truly all think about . . . sex.

Last night when we were having dinner, the subject of who would take care of me if I became very ill came up so I said first of all, do not put me in a nursing home. Charlee adamantly said "I'm not going to do that. I'll take care of you then send you to Nick's house when I get tired of you". Then I looked at D and said please don't put me in a nursing home. Where ever my feet land as in stable housing, that's where I want to die. He never gave an answer as to where he would put me if I became very ill, or very old, or incapacitated. You see, both of D's parents died in nursing homes. D's ex-wife, from information, I found out feels that D was mean to his parents for doing that and she has said to D that he treated his parents wrong in their elder years. I can't help but feel that his brother feels the same way. You see, D is extremely extremely selfish and self-serving. I've made it a point to bring that to his attention on many occasions, perhaps so he can change in certain ways. It will be for the better on both of our parts.

The conversation was fun and informative for me because as much as Charlee and me fight and argue (not physically), it is a beautiful thing to know that she's so genuine when she says she will take care of me.

Later that night, El-Haaj called me and was upset about the Facebook message Charlee left N about a month ago.

July 26, 2009:

This is a continuation of the issue with N. I had to stop writing about it because by the end of that day, about midnight, my oldest son once again had allowed his wife to somehow, once again, put it in his head that I was mistreating her. And that I was allowing Charlee to mistreat her. So many undeserving things were said about me that I couldn't allow my feelings to feel. N threatened bodily harm to Charlee if she ever saw her again. She then had her mother call me on 3-way and asked why I called her daughter a stupid bitch. N and El-Haaj were pretending not to be on the other line listening. I heard N breathing in anger when I admitted to her mother that yes, I called your daughter a stupid bitch because that's the way she was acing. And then I let Charlee speak to N's mother and explain to her what she said to N on her Facebook page. Charlee said to N (which was wrong) that she needed to grow the fuck up and let her talk to her brother. I had no idea any of this went on until two days later. El-Haaj kept calling me back to back and I wasn't answering the phone because I was running low on minutes. I finally called back. He explained to me the message Charlee sent. Fortunately, Charlee was sitting right next to me so I asked to speak to N. I had Charlee apologize. I heard N say she wants it to be like before when she and Charlee were like sisters. I apologized to N also. I then asked her how the baby was doing and school and she said everything was going fine. We said our goodbye's and I thought the whole situation was over.

Three weeks later, July 16th, after a wonderful day with D, this whole thing pops back up which brings these writings. N sends Charlee a message on July 13th saying don't ever bother or speak to her again. If she needed to speak to her brother, call him at the number she sent. And only call him in extreme emergencies. On July 16th, El-Haaj calls and asks why I'm allowing Charlee to disrespect his wife. I asked him if Charlee sent another message. He said no, it's the fact that she sent the one a month ago. "El-Haaj", I said, "I thought this was taken care of". I explained to him that I had Charlee apologize and I heard N's response that this whole issue was taken care of. He said that for N, the message brought back memories of him cheating on N, which made no damn sense to me. And I told him that N will forever hold that issue against him so she can always have power over him.

August 3, 2009:

today I have been the loneliest feeling person on earth. Monday's are still very depressing to me since being fired in May. I've tried everything to shake this sinking feeling. Maybe it's time for my menses and my hormones are fluctuating. I have had a positive day even with the depression. I've talked to two friends of mine, C and M. for the most part, they are doing fine.

The best part of my day was taking the little girl, N, that reminds me so much E out for a couple of hours. She's a little girl that Ms. H has been keeping for a while. And her mother, like me at one point when I was a young mother, has a hard time coping with a young child. I really became fond of N a couple of years ago. That's when I noticed her uncanny resemblance to my oldest daughter. I would always check on her and give her a hug. She's always looked sad, but today when we were out I now realize that N is a very happy little girl and highly intelligent. She wants to be a veterinarian or a dancer. I was very glad to hear that her mother tell her that she is a very smart little girl. And she should always say thank you when people do things for her. N is very well rounded and appreciative.

We went into several stores and she only asked for things she truly needed. She asked me questions about Nick and I told her he is with my sister for the summer. N was perturbed that the lady at S & S cafe gave her string beans instead of cabbage. She finally told me that while we were eating and then she asked me if we could walk around the plaza after we ate. That's when I was so happy to know that she's really a happy little girl. Afterward, we came to my house to pick up Charlee and she saw Charlene's room. And she had some ice cream. That was the highlight of my day. N is a truly beautiful, happy child and I hope that will follow her throughout her life.

Well, I'm getting sleepy. That's a good thing. But what got me a bit pissed off is that my apartment building all of a sudden has been having power surges, which means that in the living room the TV and fan just goes off. And I really want to sleep in the living room tonight. If I had a hammock set up on this porch, I would sleep out here. It's such a pleasant breeze out here. But ah, my crackhead neighbors are wide open. Life is amazing.

Well, I'm still feeling restless, but at the same time sleepy. I think this relationship with D may have run its course. I feel like I may be about to start wasting my time with him. He's starting to be irresponsible and I feel like he's making me word too hard when it comes to him being a man. I mean damn! He's 59 years old. He should be able to offer me more. Sex with him is old and it's the only thing that I can tolerate with him now. And that's only when I crave a human touch. Any other time I take care of me myself. It's been this way for about 6 months now. And now, it's gone downhill since Thursday. His gas was turned off. That really has gotten to me. Nothing will ever be the same with him, ever again. I feel myself about to seriously withdraw from him. I will try to sort this out the best way I can.

August 23, 2009:

Another thing, every song I listened to today made me sad: love songs, inspirational songs, message songs. They all made me think of sad things and I don't know why. Like I said earlier, I've been trying to shake it. You know what I just want to be happy, that's all I want to be; happy and fulfilled. I'm going to make sure Charlee is happy first. But after she's asleep, I'm still not happy and not fulfilled and I still don't know my purpose, my destiny. My reason for being. That's what I was feeling today. Really strong! There! I think I got it out. Now I'll try to sleep on it. I hope on the living room sofa.

August 27, 2009:

I had a very very serious talk with D. It was so unfortunate because I had to talk to him like he was Nick or El-Haaj and I told him that. I also finally told him that I was on the verge of breaking up with him do to the fact that Charlee and me went home for about 4 days and when I came over last Monday, he acted as though his world was ending . . . again.

D is constantly late for work, especially when me and Charlee are not at his house. So when I got over to his place, it was about 8:35 am This man has to be at work by 8:30 am Anyway, he had that fucked up impish look on his face like he was about to cry. I asked what was wrong. He said everything. I go home (not Charlee) and it breaks his heart because I don't tell him. Well the fact is I didn't tell him this time because I think he should know by now when I need my space. I told him that I was sorry for the lack of communication on my part. And like D tries to do before I burst his bubble is try to make it bigger than what it is. Oh, he had nightmares about being part-alien that Sunday. Then he goes on to say each time he drifted back to sleep, he would begin a new horrible dream sequence. Oh, then he dreamt that me, him, Nick, Charlee and C were caught in a race war and I had to protect him because he was not a good shot and I told him to hide in the back seat of the car. I started to laugh at him but I was really trying to be sympathetic to him until he sat down and grabbed his chest and hyperventilated. I started laughing. I mean, he was truly beyond what I could tolerate. So when I laughed, he all of a sudden tried to man up and say, "Don't push me today. I'm not in a good place, I mean it!" I looked at him and I know I had a fucked up smirk on my face because he wacked away and stood on the back porch. After that, I had nothing to say to him.

He went ahead and got ready for work and left at about 9:30 am When he left, I laughed my ass off. Needless to say, Charlee and I did not stay that night. The next morning I arrived at his place in time enough to tell him that later on that night we needed to have a long, serious talk. And like a child, he said "Can you tell me now? Don't keep me hanging." I told him that I was on the verge of breaking up with him because of how he acted yesterday. He was speechless. I told him to go to work and try not to let what I said ruin your day, which is why I wanted to wait and talk to him. That night we, or shall I say I, had a long serious talk with D. I told him the same shit I've told him before. That in this relationship, I am the stronger one and he has yet to prove to me his manliness. He tried to stare me down and I told him we can do the stare down all you want. It doesn't faze me coming from you. I told him as I have many times before that I don't do drama, but yet he's bringing it into this relationship. Also, I don't like talking to him like he's one of my children. It's a turn off. The same bullshit. Grow up, you're childish, manipulative, a turn off! His reply was that he didn't have anything to say. My reply was it really hurts to have to say these things because "at your age of 59 years, you should be teaching me how to be more adult. A 44 year old woman should not be teaching a 59 year old white male, that's been a state employee, shit." I mean, he's going through shit. Emotional shit that I went through in my 20's and 30's. Again, I told him I'm not a trained psychologist but you need fucking help and I'm not going to help you because I'm too damn old for it.

October 1, 2009:

I felt the need to write the date down because, well, I've come to a turning point with the relationship between me and D. A good point. God,

I hope it lasts! D made love to me last night like a champ. I was in pure erotic ecstasy. It's like he knew what I wanted after another one of my serious conversations with him. It started with a warm oil foot rub. This man has the softest hands I've ever felt. While he rubbed my feet, he didn't say one word, nor did I. And for the first time in a while, I found myself enjoying his touch and not wanting it to be over. I always enjoy the candle light flickering off his paintings while he rubs my feet. I felt myself gazing dreamingly at the wall, always amazed at his beautifully awesome talent. But this time it was different. It was different because of the conversation earlier that day that really started from an e-mail I sent to him that morning. The message in a nut shell said that I was tired of him not promoting his work and we missed the deadline for a major art show because he's not driven about his work. And I'm tired of him promising me things just to keep me hanging on. His pathetic rebuttal, by email reply, was love should be forever whether in a cardboard box or mansion. And he's not ready to show his work because he doesn't think it's good enough. He goes on to say that art is done because artists like to do art, not for the money. Van goh went crazy for his art and died broke.

When D arrived home, I was at the park walking. I didn't want to see him and was heavily debating on going home after Charlee and I ate dinner. But as I walked in the park, I felt that he had replied to my email with exactly the words he wrote. I walked in the door and I hugged him until he responded back to me. He didn't want to. That's when I read his reply and that's when we had our serious conversation. D began to rub my upper thigh. Then he stopped, came to the head of the bed, and kissed me soft and passionate, almost teasingly. Then I responded wantingly and was surprised at myself. He then went back to rubbing my feet, still not saying a word. I began to wonder if he was teasing me, trying to teach me a lesson because of our conversation. I had to get D to understand that this relationship is over if he doesn't start making good on his promises.

I whispered that it felt good. I wanted to be the first to say something. Then he said it felt good to him too to rub my feet. Then we fell back into silence again. He began to rub my upper thigh again. I was so tryin to fight the sensation. I've always noticed that a moan will reveal itself no matter how I try to fight it. And for D that's all he needed to hear for the approval, to start stroking me with his fingers and drive me absolutely crazy. And man was it working. I wanted to give D absolute control of me, so I turned on my tummy. Still, there were no words said. He kissed me everywhere a girl could be kissed. And I started crying, to myself. He was killing me in a good way. I finally spoke again, telling him I was tired of being in control and I wanted to give him complete control of me tonight.

October 9, 2009:

Charlee and me have been home all week and we came back today. It's D's birthday this weekend and I'm going to try and make it as special as I can. I'm going to have to break it to him that we're going home on Sunday. You see, when I go home for a while, I do admit I get very selfish. I really like and need my own space and a lot of times, D really crowds me.

October 21, 2009:

D's b-day weekend was great. The weather was outstanding. High 70's. I treated him to taste of Atlanta on Saturday, then the Chandler Park Arts Festival on Sunday. Charlee and I went home Sunday and of course, he was devastated. We stayed at our home in the West-end for an entire week and I loved it. We both did.

The weather is starting to become quite cool and I know I'm not going to be able to afford my electric bill. Especially not being employed. Last year at this time I was gainfully employed, but could not afford $300.00 plus electric bills and we ended up at D's for 5 months.

D has expressed to me that he wants us to live as a family because he has no idea what I'm doing when we go home to the West-end. He goes on to say a whole lot of the same bullshit. He's said every time we have these serious talks. He actually thinks I'm having an affair with P. I think this time D knows I will leave him and never come back. I had to be blunt with him again and let him know that I don't need to be around him constantly. I need my own space and yes, he crowds me. I cannot offer him what he needs at this time because I'm not ready to. And he's still trying to possess me. What I didn't tell him is that he makes it really hard for me to want to make love to him because he can be such a bitch.

I mean damn! How many times does a woman have to tell a man she feels more like the man in the relationship. I miss making love the way D an I used to and the frequency of it. I'm having trouble getting it back. I am starting to long for other companionship. I'm starting to think about W quite often, and also starting to act as though I'm single. Yesterday I got so much attention and phone numbers passed to me. I really felt very womanly. I'm determined to be a good girl though. But it's getting kind of hard. But at the same time fun because everybody is out for pussy or money. I have the pussy, but I'm the broke bitch right now living off of $330.00 a week.

November 7, 2009:

Today is absolutely beautiful. It's about 72 degrees. Everybody is out doing their own thing. There are a lot of motorcyclists out. I, for one, had to do laundry. I've found this really cool eclectic spot in midtown called Laundry Lounge. It's very hidden. I happened to find it looking for a way around a parking lot. It's truly a lounge, complete with a coffee maker, magazine rack, soft rock music playing, a beautiful view, nice lounge chairs and tables. All of this is set in the back area. The video games are at the entrance. They have my favorite game, Galaga. It's very soothing and comfortable in this place and I really feel like I'm getting away from society when I do my laundry here.

I've finally broken up with D. Break-ups are never the way they are on TV. There was no other woman and no other man. It was D being a drama queen. He finally crossed the line when he lied on Charlee. On the morning of November 2nd, I decided to have some time to myself. I got up, took a shower, left, and went out to a beautiful restaurant with C and A. the restaurant was quite crowded but I had enough time to get back to mid-town at about 12:30. the time D and I agreed on. Well, I forgot they were going to block streets off in the midtown area. I didn't get to D's apartment until 1:15. he left a dry note letting me know where he was going to be viewing the parade. I got my lawn chair, asked Charlee if she wanted to go and she said no, so I left.

November 17, 2009:

Well, it's finally over tonight. I'm going to tell D that we are going to be friends starting tonight. I'm going to ask him about the paintings that are the likeness of me, if I can purchase them or outright have them. I don't know how to even begin to describe how to explain his final selfish stupidity that has nailed the coffin shut. As I absorb everything, all I'm feeling right now is sickness to my stomach. And when things start to make me sick, it's time for those things to take their place in a file. To be laughed about down the line as I continue to grow and learn.

April 29, 2010:

It's amazing how surroundings look and feel when you have music in your ear. Everyone is doing their own thing, you can't hear them which is the purpose of having music in ones ear. The world appears to be a peaceful place, especially when the sun is shinning. I'm listening to a variety of music right now. It's Stevie Wonder (if you really love me). It's really hitting the spot. Not because I'm in love, but because love hurts like a bitch. D is a sick bitch and C.J.'s bullshit caught up with him. D is a bitch once again. The drama queen in him reared its ugly head. Charlee went to her Dad's house last Saturday evening. Thursday and Friday, we as a quasi-family, had a great time. D and me had a movie night while Charlee was in the room having teenage time on the phone, computer, and looking at a movie at the same time. So Saturday, when she left for her dad's house, D and me had dinner and a great conversation at about 9:45 pm I excused myself for bed. D immediately became angry.

About two hours later, I got up to use the bathroom. He got up too and asked if I was okay. Yes, I have a little tummy ache from eating beef (which I don't eat much of anymore). He explained that he wasn't going with me on Sunday to V's because he felt as though I didn't want to be bothered with him. I immediately interjected and told him that I didn't know where his thoughts were coming from and that I was going back to bed. He then asked, in a whinny, shaky voice, "Why don't you want to hold me?" I was sickened and repulsed by him. He looked and sounded like a weak ass woman or a damn fagot. I wanted to straight bitch slap him. I was so fucking repulsed by him. I just closed the door and shook my head wondering where the hell his manhood could be. As of this writing, I am absolutely repulsed by D. I mean I can't believe how fucking feminine he is. Words cannot express the disgust. I feel for this man. I can't even finish writing how I feel about other things that have gone on good and bad that now fucking disappointed I am in D. I mean, how much of a bitch can he turn into?

December 3, 2010:

I'm sure that I'm not the only woman in the world and throughout history that has lost total physical interest in her male partner. This has happened to me twice in my adult life. C.J. Because he couldn't get it up and when he did, it lasted about one minute. That is a cliché I used to hear on TV, but I'll be damned if it's not true. And D, not because he can't get it up but because of the things I wrote last in this journal. I wrote that he finally sealed the nail in the coffin. Well he did. For 8 months I have been forcing myself to be physical with him, praying for when its over. I can't do it anymore. I had to tell him today how I felt.

December 20, 2010:

I always knew the bitch had it in him. A man just doesn't hit a woman all of the sudden. They've done it before. D finally lost it on me. Not because I called him a name, but because he took me to that level again, talking about how he's going to become erratic and not know what he is going to do. Because me and him are not being intimate.

January 12, 2011:

I haven't been sleeping well at all. Last night I felt as though something was crawling on me and biting me. I know it's my nerves. I am very unhappy with the situation I have gotten myself into. I feel as though the final failure has occurred. The failure of the fact that I failed myself. I didn't follow my own rule when it came to a relationship. And now I feel truly hopelessly stuck and fucked. I have no job, no money, no prospects of a job or money, and no place of my own. Oh my God! How did this happen? What answers am I supposed to receive through constant failures and fights that I've never won? I have never won a fight when it was something I knew was wrong towards me. Never! How many times am I supposed to fall and get back up. I'm not even sure if I'm stronger when I get back up. I always feel more hatred for my fellow man. Especially the white man. It's so wrong for me to be this way. I've actually known people feeling the way I feel now and chastised them for their hatred of the white man. But now, more than ever, I understand the harshness of that hate.

The white man cannot be trusted. He is the devil. They lure you in with the false promises. But the minute you show him that you are free with your mind and body, you will suffer the consequences of his white power. I have now experienced this evilness first hand. I should have known better. If the white man treats his own white wife with brutal and cruel forces, what the hell made me think he would treat me better. You know what the answer is to that? His white skin!

Black men have done their women so wrong due to what the white man has done to him. The black man no longer knows how to treat his woman. Therefore, leaving the black woman bitter towards the black man, causing the black woman to find the white man in her mind a more desirable mate. The whole damn thing is just wrong and unbalanced. I feel so lost right now. My brother has given me bible verses to read. I'm so afraid to believe in God because I don't feel he exists. I know he does but I don't feel it. I feel as though God has let me down. And every time I've felt this way, it's because man has let me down. When I learn to let go and let God, I will release Man. I'm slowly learning, I am. It just hurts so bad to know that man, no matter how much you try to trust him and believe in him, you are let down every time. Maybe I'm strange. I just think man should be good to one another and expect nothing in return.

November 7, 2011:

Today is my little cousins birthday, Dy. He's 21 years old. I hope I get to speak to him on the phone. Facebook can be so impersonal sometimes. I'm going to start doing what my mom used to do and mail cards.

I started out on this writing journey today extremely melancholy. Still, I'm not sure what to write. However, I did read some pages of my past thoughts and I'm very pleased to know that my relationship with D is a thousand times better and I truly love him. And I'm in love with him. Unfortunately, it's still hard for me to verbally express it.

I talk to my brother quite often. He gives me beautiful advice. He's such a spiritual person. I wish I could be like him. But I struggle with some unknown force that I can't control sometimes. The force of trying to make people do right, to be fair to one another, to just show love, compassion, fairness, equality. Those have been my battles. And each time I lose in my mind horribly. I've got to stop and let things play out.

I've put my foot in my mouth once again, thinking I was doing the right thing. And I balded up the schedule at work. Nobody saw me do it. But the manager told a captain to write a statement about it.

You see, simple and dumb shit like that that I get myself into. Then I start to agonize and torment myself over it. Alex told me I can only make things important and bring attention to it if I say anything.

As God as my witness, I so want this to blow over, but I'm scared again. And I feel stupid as fuck. I'm literally feeling sorry for myself about this stupid situation, but I did it! I did it!

I don't know how to talk to God anymore because I've been questioning existence of God. I don't know if that's right or wrong. I certainly don't want anything tragic to happen to anyone associated with me to know God exists.

That's whats been tormenting me for a long time now. God and his existence. It seems as though when I thought I was feeling God and would get happy and praise him, shit would hit the fan. Until finally, I stopped. I stopped reading the Bible, I stopped praying, going to church. I even started referring to God as a "Higher Power".

This is how utterly confused I am. It scares me something awful. I mean, I need to believe in something good, something beautiful, and untouched . . . pure. I don't know what that is anymore. Does this mean I'm afraid of God or Jesus like the young fellow is at Caribou Coffee? I don't think it is.

I believe that man has severely tainted what I thought and think about God, Jesus, the Holy Ghost (or Spirit). They are supposed to represent and mean something. That's what scares me. And that's why I try to change people into doing the right thing and it back-fires every single time.

There is this song that I listen to periodically. He's an one-time God, yes he is. I know that to be true, I do. I just have to start believing it again.

January 11, 2012:

Well, I lost another job. Long story, it ended badly! I called MN a house nigga and told him when they get through with his black ass, they are going to hang him. And that, if my last check wasn't right, I was gonna blow their muthafuckin asses up. So I've been CT.'d from going to Peachtree Center Mall.

The Lords Prayer: Our Father, which art in heaven, hallowed be thy name. They kingdom come. They will be done. In earth, as it is in heaven.

Give us this day our daily bread. And forgive us our debts, as we forgive our debtors. And lead us not into temptation, but deliver us from evil: for thine is the kingdom, the power, and the glory, forever. Amen! Matthew 6:9-13

Depression—psychopathol. An abnormal state of inactivity and unpleasant emotion, as in manic-depressive insanity.

Possessed—influenced or controlled as by evil spirits, ones passions, a fixed idea. Mad; crazed.

Schizophrenia—a type of psychosis characterized by loss of contact with environment and by disintegration of personality.

Schizothymia—a schizoid condition or temperament remaining within the bounds of normality.

www.ingramcontent.com/pod-product-compliance
Lightning Source LLC
Chambersburg PA
CBHW020306290526
45784CB00003B/1389